101 WAYS TO

stitch | craft
create

QUICK & EASY PROJECTS TO
STITCH, SEW, KNIT, BEAD & FOLD

D&C
David and Charles

www.stitchcraftcreate.com

A DAVID & CHARLES BOOK
© F&W Media International, Ltd 2012

David & Charles is an imprint of F&W Media International, Ltd
Brunel House, Forde Close, Newton Abbot, TQ12 4PU, UK

F&W Media International, Ltd is a subsidiary of F+W Media, Inc
10151 Carver Road, Cincinnati OH45242, USA

A catalogue record for this book is available from the British Library.

ISBN-13: 978-1-4463-0187-6 paperback
ISBN-10: 1-4463-0187-7 paperback

ISBN-13: 978-1-4463-0282-8 hardback
ISBN-10: 1-4463-0282-2 hardback

Printed in China by RR Donnelley for
F&W Media International, Ltd
Brunel House, Forde Close, Newton Abbot, TQ12 4PU, UK

10 9 8 7 6 5 4 3 2 1

Acquisitions Editor: Sarah Callard
Desk Editor: Jeni Hennah
Project Editor: Cheryl Brown
Design Consultant: Prudence Rogers
Senior Designer: Victoria Marks
Photographer: Sian Irvine
Senior Production Controller: Kelly Smith

F+W Media publishes high quality books on a wide range of subjects.
For more great book ideas visit: **www.rucraft.co.uk**

CONTENTS

APPLIQUÉ & EMBROIDERY

SAILING BOAT LAVENDER BAG
by Jenny Arnott

You Will Need:

Fabric for lavender bag front
and back:
Two pieces 11cm x 14cm
(4⅜in x 5½in)
Free Spirit Designer Solids Ice and
Kaffe Fassett Spot China Blue

◆

Scraps of fabric for appliqué
Tilda Red Stripe, Tanya Whelan
Delilah Dots Red and Kaffe
Fassett Spot China Blue

◆

Blue and red sewing thread
Gutermann colours 13 and 156

◆

Blue polka dot ribbon

◆

Dried lavender

1. Using the templates, cut a boat base and flag from red spotty material. Cut one sail from stripy fabric, and another from blue spotty fabric.

2. Position the appliqué pieces onto the front fabric. Machine stitch around the edge of each piece in contrasting thread. Go over your stitch lines two or three times to add definition.

3. Cut a 14cm (5½in) length of blue polka dot ribbon. Pin the front and back pieces right sides facing, with the ribbon hanging down inside between them from the centre of the top edge.

4. With a 6mm (¼in) seam allowance, stitch all around the edge of the bag, leaving a 6cm (2⅜in) gap on the bottom edge. Reinforce the stitching by the opening.

5. Turn the lavender bag right side out and press with a medium heat. Fill with scented lavender, then neatly stitch the gap closed.

FLOWER GIRL HOOP
by Kirsty Neale

You Will Need:

Ivory 32-count linen

◆

Grey and red
stranded cotton (floss)
DMC colours 413 and 304

◆

Wooden embroidery hoop

◆

Decorative tape
Cath Kidston

◆

Flower punch
McGill Mixed Baby Bloom

◆

Patterned papers
Cath Kidston stationery box

◆

White felt

1. Stretch and secure the linen fabric in your embroidery hoop. Wrap decorative tape around the sides of the hoop, then fold over and press down onto the front edges to decorate.

2. Draw or trace a head and shoulders onto the fabric using a vanishing marker pen. Sew over the lines with backstitch, using just two or three strands of grey (DMC 413) to keep the lines fine and clear.

3. Punch out tiny flowers from a selection of coloured papers. Arrange them on your original drawing or tracing to make a fun flowered hat. Once you're happy with the arrangement, lift them off one at a time, and fix each to your fabric with a single small cross stitch.

4. Trim away excess fabric at the back of your hoop. Cut a circle of felt to fit over the back, and glue it in place to hide the wrong side of your stitching.

APPLIQUÉ & EMBROIDERY

BIRD MP3 PLAYER CASE
by Marion Elliot

You Will Need:

Fabric for case and lining:
Two pieces 40cm x 10cm
(15½in x 3⅞in)
Free Spirit Designer Solids Orchid
and Amy Butler Soul Blossoms
Laurel Dots Periwinkle

◆

Scraps of fabric for appliqué
Amy Butler Soul Blossoms

◆

**White and black
sewing thread**
Gutermann colours 800 and 000

◆

**Fusible webbing and
wadding (batting)**

◆

Ribbon, bead and clip ring

1. Trace all the pieces of the bird and branch motifs onto fusible webbing and cut out roughly. Iron them onto your chosen appliqué fabrics and cut out neatly.

2. Remove the backing paper from the motifs and position them, glue side down, onto the top half of the main fabric. Iron into place. Machine stitch around the motifs using a medium stitch and contrasting thread to appliqué them to the fabric.

3. Iron on a lightweight wadding to the back of the main fabric, and fold the main fabric in half with right sides facing. Insert and pin a loop of ribbon between the side seams, facing inwards.

4. Using a 1cm (⅜in) seam allowance, machine stitch around the sides and bottom edge to within 3cm (1⅛in) of the top edge, to make the case. Repeat for the lining fabric. Turn the case through to the right side but not the lining.

5. Insert the case into the lining. Pin and machine stitch the top edge of the case and lining together, right sides facing. Leave a 1.5cm (⅝in) gap above the top of the side seam at either side. Turn lining through to the inside.

6. Machine stitch a 1.5cm (⅝in) wide channel across the front and back of the case and thread ribbon through it. Thread on the bead and knot the ribbon ends. Attach a clip to the ribbon loop.

DITSY HEART HAIRCLIP
by Nicola Langdon

You Will Need:

Purple felt

◆

Gold, magenta, purple and
blue stranded cotton (floss)
DMC colours E3852, 309, 327 and 792

◆

Flower button

◆

Scrap of floral fabric (optional)
Amy Butler Soul Blossoms
Sari Bloom Raspberry

◆

Hairclip

1. Using the heart template, cut two hearts from purple felt. Machine stitch three rambling stems onto one of the hearts with a small straight stitch and gold thread; finish off the ends. Hand sew small leaves and petals randomly onto the gold stems using a small running stitch.

2. Using one strand of magenta, embroider a tulip at the top of the centre stem – outline with running stitch and fill with satin stitch to fill. Finish off ends.

3. Now outline the tulip flower with one strand of purple stranded cotton and a small running stitch. Using a longer running stitch, add four or five stitches to the base of the flower.

4. Cut a small ditsy flower from your floral fabric scrap. Stitch to the left stem with small neat stitches in the centre. Do not worry if the edges fray a little as this looks even better! Use gold thread to sew the flower button at the top of the right stem.

5. Place the second heart behind the first and tack (baste) into place. This will hide your finishings. Using one strand of blue stranded cotton, machine stitch together using a small straight stitch 2mm (³⁄₃₂in) from the edge. Alternatively hand sew with a small running stitch Finish the ends. Finally, oversew the homespun heart to the hairclip.

APPLIQUÉ & EMBROIDERY

CHRISTMAS PUDDING TREE DECORATION

by Sue Trevor

You Will Need:

Brown, green and white felt

◆

Red felt embellishments

◆

White, brown and green sewing thread
Gutermann colours 1, 767 and 396

◆

Red stranded cotton (floss)
DMC colour 349

◆

Polyester wadding (batting)

1. Cut one 23cm (9in) diameter circle and one 4cm (1½in) diameter circle from brown felt. Using the templates, cut three holly leaves from green felt and one icing piece from white felt.

2. Hand sew the white icing piece to the centre of the large brown circle using white sewing thread. Make a hanging loop with red stranded cotton by sewing through the middle of the icing and back through again, then knotting the ends together on the inside.

3. Hand sew around the large brown circle with running stitch, about 3mm (⅛in) from the edge, using brown sewing thread. Pull your stitches tightly to gather the felt as you go.

4. With the needle and thread on the outside, stuff the felt with polyester wadding and pull the gathers tightly to form a spherical pudding shape. Stitch at the bottom to hold in place. Neatly sew the smaller circle of felt over the base to finish.

5. Embroider the centre of the holly leaves with running stitch using green sewing thread. Sew the holly leaves and red felt embellishments to the top using the red stranded cotton and green sewing thread.

APPLIQUÉ & EMBROIDERY

COTTAGE TEA COSY
by Marion Elliot

You Will Need:

Fabric for tea cosy front, back and lining:
Two pieces 35cm x 30cm (13⅞in x 11⅞in)
Two pieces 35cm x 25cm (13⅞in x 9⅞in)
Tilda Molly Pink, Free Spirit Designer Solids Barberry and Chartreuse

◆

Scraps of fabric for appliqué

◆

Black and cream sewing thread

◆

Fusible webbing and wadding (batting)

◆

Ribbon and buttons

1. Trace and transfer the tea cosy templates to your chosen fabrics and cut out the front, back and linings.

2. Trace and transfer the roof, windows and doors to fusible webbing; cut out roughly. Iron onto your chosen fabrics and cut out neatly. Remove the backing paper and position the motifs, glue side down, onto the cosy front. Iron in place. Machine stitch around the motifs using a medium stitch and contrasting thread.

3. Sew crosses on the windows to represent panes of glass. Sew lines across the roof for tiles, and down the door for panels.

4. Pin the cosy front and the cosy back to the wadding; cut out and machine stitch using a 1cm (⅜in) seam allowance. Pin front and back together, right sides facing. Insert and pin a loop of ribbon between the top seams, facing inwards. Machine stitch together, using a 1cm (⅜in) seam allowance. Trim the seams and turn through.

5. Pin the lining front and back together and machine stitch around the sides using a 1cm (⅜in) seam allowance. Leave the lining wrong side out, and pull it over the cosy, then pin, matching side seams and lower raw edges.

6. Machine stitch around the lower edge of the cosy, leaving a 10cm (3⅞in) gap at the back. Turn through to the right side and slip stitch the gap closed. Sew a button to the door for a handle and to the base of the ribbon loop.

RUSSIAN DOLL DECORATION
by Kirsty Neale

You Will Need:

Pink, brown, blue and lime felt

◆

Scraps of patterned fabric
Tilda Berrie Teal, Tilda Christmas
House Grandma Rose Red
and Amy Butler Lotus Full
Moon Polka Dot Lime

◆

Scraps of cream fabric

◆

**Grey, red, green, teal and
pink stranded cotton (floss)**
DMC colours 413, 304, 166, 518 and 601

◆

Decorative ribbons
Tilda Fruit Garden

◆

Toy filling

1. Cut out pattern pieces, as noted on the Russian doll template. Position face and hair over each body section, and tack (baste) around the edges. Mark then stitch eyes, nose and mouth, using a single strand of grey (DMC 413) and red (DMC 304) .

2. Place the cape on top and sew together with running stitch around the edge of the face and the curved bottom edges.

3. Place the doll front on top of the doll back, right sides facing. Cut a ribbon length of and fold it in half for a hanging loop. Sandwich the ribbon ends in between the front and back at the top of the head.

4. Sew a running stitch around the outside edges to join the front and back together. Stop sewing 2cm–3cm (¾in x 1⅛in) before you reach your start point but don't cut off your thread just yet.

5. Feed a small amount of toy filling through the gap. Use a pencil or knitting needle to push it right up into the head, and down into the bottom corners. Don't be tempted to overstuff! Continue to stitch the gap closed, then knot and trim excess thread.

APPLIQUÉ & EMBROIDERY

GADGET CASE
by Jeni Hennah

You Will Need:

Red, purple, blue, cream and grey felt

◆

White stranded cotton (floss)
DMC colour BLANC

◆

Buttons

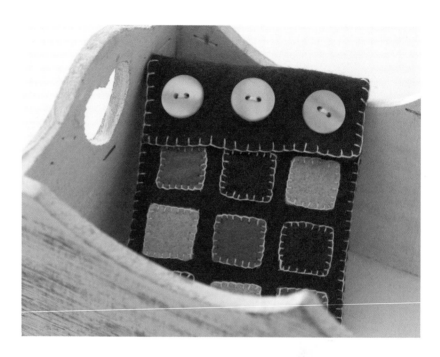

1. Measure the object that you want the case to hold. Cut three rectangles of red felt: two front pieces measuring approximately 2cm (¾in) more than the object's width and length, and one back piece measuring 2cm (¾in) more than the object's width and 5cm (2in) more than the object's length. For example, if the object measures 5cm x 10cm (2in x 3⅞in), the front pieces will measure 7cm x 12cm (2¾in x 4¾in) and the back piece will measure 7cm x 15cm (2¾in x 6in).

2. Cut out twelve 2cm (¾in) squares in different colours of felt to decorate the front of the case.

3. Attach the felt squares to one of the front pieces by sewing with blanket stitch using two strands of white stranded cotton (DMC BLANC).

4. Decide which of the shorter sides of the decorated front piece will be the 'top' and sew buttons to the squares at this end.

5. Pin the second front piece to the back of the decorated piece. Blanket stitch along the 'top' side (one of the shorter sides that will become the top of the inside of the case) using two strands of white stranded cotton (DMC BLANC).

6. Pin the back piece to the two front pieces, ensuring that the overlap is at the 'top' and that the decorated front piece is on the outside. Cut small slits at the top of the back piece above each button and check that the buttons can be pulled through easily.

7. Blanket stitch around the outside of the whole case using two strands of white stranded cotton (DMC BLANC), removing the pins as you work around. The two front pieces should be completely sewn together and a pocket should be created between the second front piece and the back piece.

APPLIQUÉ & EMBROIDERY

SEWING PATTERN TIDY
by Charlotte Addison

You Will Need:

Fabric for tidy
Dena Fishbein Kumari Garden
Tarika Moss and Free Spirit
Designer Pinwheels Yale Blue

◆

Fabric for appliqué
Dena Fishbein Kumari
Garden Tarika Moss

◆

White sewing thread
Gutermann colour 800

◆

Silk ribbon and button

◆

Medium fusible interlining

1. Measure the width and the height of the front, back and depth of the sewing patterns. Add 2.5cm (1in) all around for the seam allowance, and allowing a little extra room, cut out two pieces of fabric to this size, one for the top and one for the lining.

2. Using the template, cut out a sewing machine from lining fabric and another from the interlining. With the top fabric facing right side up, iron and sew the appliqué centred at the right-hand side.

3. Place the lining fabric on top, right sides facing, and machine stitch around the edge leaving a 5cm (2in) gap. Trim corners. Turn right side out, press and sew gap closed. Attach button to the appliqué.

4. Fold the cover in half and measure the height and three-quarters of the width of the front cover and add a 2.5cm (1in) seam allowance. Cut two pieces of lining fabric to this size for the flaps. Hem one edge on each flap.

5. Lay the cover flat with the right side facing up. Pin the flaps at either side, with right sides facing, so that the hemmed edges are facing the centre.

6. Place a long piece of ribbon (for fastening) between the cover and the left flap so that the ribbon will be level with the button of your appliquéd sewing machine. Machine stitch around the three outside edges of each flap. Trim corners, turn right side out, and press.

APPLIQUÉ & EMBROIDERY

STITCHED LAVENDER BAG
by Ali Burdon

You Will Need:

White cotton fabric for bag:
Two pieces 11cm x 11cm
(4⅜in x 4⅜in)

◆

Stranded cotton (floss)
in a variety of colours

◆

Medium fusible interlining:
Two pieces 11cm x 11cm
(4⅜in x 4⅜in)

◆

24cm (9½in) red ric-rac
Tilda

◆

Dried lavender

1. Iron the interlining onto the wrong sides of the fabric pieces following the manufacturer's instructions.

2. Using a dressmaker's pencil or pen, mark a grid in the centre of the right side of one of the pieces of fabric, making the lines around 6mm (¼in) apart.

3. Set your sewing machine to make a satin stitch 2mm in length and 0.5mm in width; stitch along the **inner** lines of your grid.

4. Work across the grid from left to right, and without cutting the thread between the lines, turn the fabric through 90 degrees and work across the grid from left to right the other way. Finally sew round the outer edge of the grid (this will hide all the uncut threads) and fasten off.

5. Use different coloured stranded cotton to sew cross stitches in the grid squares, using three strands in the needle. It is not necessary to cut the thread between stitches, but don't pull it too tight or you will pucker the fabric.

6. Fasten off each colour set of stitches by taking your needle and thread through the back of a couple of grid stitches.

7. Fold the ric-rac in half and pin to the corner of the decorated fabric square, loop pointing down. Place the other fabric square on top, right sides facing; machine stitch together with a 1cm (⅜in) seam allowance leaving a 4cm (1½in) turning gap. Trim seam to 6mm (¼in) and trim corners. Turn right side out, press, and stuff with lavender. Sew the gap closed with an invisible ladder stitch.

APPLIQUÉ TREES CUSHION

by Kirsty Neale

You Will Need:

Fabric for cushion front
and back:
One piece 40cm x 40cm
(15½in x 15½in)
Two pieces 40cm x 23cm
(15½in x 9in)
Tilda Winterbird Big Spot Blue

◆

Scraps of fabric for appliqué
Heather Bailey Nicey Jane Slim
Dandy Pink and Picnic Bouquet
Gold, Tanya Whelan Delilah
Amelie White and Amy Butler Soul
Blossoms Disco Flower Chocolate

◆

Sewing thread

◆

Fusible webbing

1. Decorate the cushion front with the simple appliqué design. Iron fusible webbing onto the reverse side of three contrasting fabrics. Draw three circles freehand and cut out. Cut out three tree trunk shapes from fusible-webbing backed striped fabric. Peel off the backing paper, and iron the circles onto the cushion front with trunk beneath each.

2. Machine stitch around the edges of the appliqué to hold each piece more securely in place.

3. To make the envelope back, first fold over and stitch a narrow double hem down one long edge of each cushion back piece.

4. With right sides facing, pin the hemmed rectangles to the cushion front with the hemmed edges overlapping. Machine stitch together around the sides. Remove the pins, then trim the corners to reduce bulk. Turn your finished cushion cover the right way out through the envelope back.

5. Gently push each corner into shape using a knitting needle. Press the seams flat for a neat finish. Insert a cushion pad (35cm x 35cm/14in x 14in).

APPLIQUÉ & EMBROIDERY

FELT ADVENT CALENDAR

by Charlotte Addison

You Will Need:

Ruby, green, baby blue, grey and white felt

◆

Dark blue stranded cotton (floss)
DMC colour 939

◆

3m (3¼yd) brown hemp cord

◆

12 buttons

1. Cut out 25 2.5cm (1in) squares in white felt. Number each 1 to 24, and embroider the numbers in backstitch using two strands of dark blue stranded cotton (DMC 939) .

2. Using the templates cut out 12 pairs of hearts and 12 pairs of birds from the ruby, green, baby blue and grey felt (six pairs from each colour). Sew the numbered squares onto one of each pair, alternating between hearts and birds.

3. Take the un-numbered hearts and birds and pin them to their matching numbered pair. You should end up with 12 hearts and 12 birds, numbered 1 to 24.

4. Make a loop with the first 35.5cm (14in) of cord and knot. Thread the unlooped end through a tapestry needle. Thread through the shape numbered 1 from the top and pull through until it is at the looped end; knot the cord to secure. Leave 4cm (1½in) and knot the cord again.

5. Thread on the remaining shapes in numerical order (2, 3, 4, etc), making knots in between each as in step 4. To finish, trim any excess cord and embellish the hearts by sewing on a button at the top of each. Mark the day with a little wooden peg.

APPLIQUÉ & EMBROIDERY

HOT WATER BOTTLE COVER
by Ellen Kharade

You Will Need:

Lime, turquoise and
white wool felt

◆

Green/blue sequins and
lime green seed beads

◆

White sewing thread
Gutermann colour 800

1. Trace and transfer the hot water bottle cover patterns to the turquoise wool felt fabric and cut out.

2. Using the template cut out a star from the lime green wool felt fabric. Cut a 6cm (2⅜in) diameter circle from turquoise wool felt.

3. Pin the star to the centre of the cover front and machine stitch around the motif using a zigzag stitch. Pin the turquoise circle to the star and machine stitch into place using a straight stitch in a spiral pattern.

4. Sew seed beads over the circle motif and sequins to the points of the star.

5. Cut out a 4.5cm (1⅝in) diameter circle from the white wool felt and a 2.5cm (1in) diameter circle from the turquoise wool felt. Pin into place below the star and machine stitch around the outside of the white circle using a zigzag stitch.

6. Change to a straight stitch and machine stitch around the turquoise circle in a spiral pattern. Repeat to make a second circle motif and stitch in place above the star motif.

7. To make the envelope back, fold over and pin a 1cm (⅜in) hem along the straight edges of the two back pieces. With right sides facing, pin the back pieces to the cover front with the hemmed edges overlapping at the centre. Machine stitch together around the edges. Turn the hot water bottle cover the right side out and press.

DINKY SAIL BOAT BROOCH
by Nicola Langdon

You Will Need:

Baby blue felt

◆

Scrap of patterned fabric
Amy Butler Soul Blossoms
Sari Bloom Raspberry

◆

Metallic turquoise,
blue, pink and red
stranded cotton (floss)
DMC colours E334, 803, 3733 and 321

◆

Lilac, red and yellow
silk ribbons

◆

Brooch fixing

1. Using the template cut two boats from blue felt. Using metallic turquoise thread hand-sew waves to the bottom of one boat 5mm (³⁄₁₆in) from the edge. Add four or five randomly-placed running stitches for sea-spray. Finish off the ends.

2. Cut and appliqué a patterned fabric triangle to the sail. Using one strand of blue stranded cotton, machine stitch along the edge of the sail. Use running stitch, 2mm (³⁄₃₂in) from the sail edge. Finish off ends.

3. Using alternate blue and pink stranded cotton, machine or hand-sew five lines across the sail. Start in the bottom-left corner and sew out using a small running stitch. Finish off ends.

4. Cut a length of lilac and red ribbon approximately 5cm (2in) long. Tack (baste) the ribbon to the top of the boat below the sail. Using lilac or red thread, machine or hand-stitch along the ribbon to secure. Ensure the ribbon ends are tucked underneath.

5. Cut a length of yellow ribbon, approximately 2cm (³⁄₄in) long. Fold in half and sew behind the top-left of the sail. Finish all ends and 'V' the ribbon-ends.

6. Place the second felt boat at the back of the decorated boat to hide the finished ends and tack (baste) together. Using one strand of blue stranded cotton, machine or hand-sew around the edge of the boats to join together as in step 2. Oversew the boat to a brooch fixing to finish.

APPLIQUÉ & EMBROIDERY

EMBROIDERED BUTTON HEADS
by Kirsty Neale

You Will Need:

29mm stainless steel
cover buttons

◆

Black, red and grey
stranded cotton (floss)
DMC colours 310, 666 and 413

◆

Scraps of cream fabric
Free Spirit Designer Solids Sand Dune

◆

Brown felt

1. Using a vanishing fabric marker, draw around your button onto a piece of thin card, and cut out. Use the card circle as a template, and trace around it onto cream fabric. Draw a face inside the circle.

2. Embroider over the details of the face with one or two strands of the stranded cotton. Use a small backstitch, with French knots for details like eyes or freckles.

3. Cut out any extra pieces, for example hair from brown felt, or fabric or ribbon to make bows. Glue or stitch into place.

4. Trim the cream fabric into a circle a little larger all around than the marked face. Sew a gathering stitch around the edges. Place the button face down in the centre, and pull the thread ends to gather the fabric around it. Tie a knot to secure.

5. Push the back piece of the button into place to hold everything together and hide the raw edges. Use your finished buttons on clothing and papercraft projects, or attach to jewellery findings to make a cute brooch, hairclip or ring.

BEADING

CHARMING BRACELET
by Dorothy Wood

You Will Need:

Beads
The Bead Café

◆

Silver lobster claw clasp

◆

Silver headpins

◆

Silver jump rings

◆

50cm (20in) silver chain

1. Cut a length of chain twice the circumference of your wrist plus 2cm–3cm (¾in–1⅛in) for ease. Using flat-nose pliers open a jump ring and loop through a second jump ring and one end of the chain. Close the jump ring. Use another jump ring to attach the lobster claw clasp to the other end.

2. Sort the beads into individual types ready to attach eight small groups of beads along the length of chain. Note: it is better to lay the chain flat and attach the beads to the same side of the chain so that they all hang attractively when worn.

3. Count out eight clear faceted beads with loops. Arrange along the chain so that they are equally spaced attaching each one with a jump ring.

4. So that the beads are mixed when the chain is wrapped around twice, you need to attach beads in a fairly regular pattern to one half of the chain and then attach the beads on the other side in a mirror image. Arrange the beads to your preference.

5. Repeat to attach other beads with loops again using jump rings. For beads with holes, insert a headpin, bend over at right angles and trim the end to 7mm (⁹⁄₃₂in). Use round-nose pliers to bend into a loop. Open the loop and attach to the chain then close the loop again.

6. Check the bead arrangement on your bracelet by wrapping the chain round your wrist. Make any necessary adjustments.

BEADING

EMBROIDERED WRIST CUFF
by Laura Whitcher

You Will Need:

8mm Topaz glass
faceted beads

◆

Nine shades of red, orange,
yellow and green
stranded cotton (floss)
Assorted DMC colours

◆

Two birthstone beads
A Bead At A Time

1. Select nine shades of
stranded cotton in yellow, orange,
red and green. Measure a length of
each colour to 3m (3¼yd), cut and
fold in half. Gather all together and
tie a knot. Plait 3cm (1⅛in) and then
add a birthstone bead. Arrange the
colours in your desired formation,
laying out in the same order twice.

2. Take the thread that is second
in from the right, double knot it over
thread on the right. Take the thread
now third from the right and double
knot over each of the threads on
the right. Do this for all threads
until all moved to the far right.

3. Place a bead onto six of the
threads; evenly space.Take the
thread second from the left, double
knot over the thread on the left.
Work all of the threads in this way
until all have moved to the far left.

4. Repeat steps 2 and 3. Place
beads on six threads (you should
have three rows of beads now).

5. Gather threads, keeping
beads in place, and plait. Place a
birthstone bead onto the plaited
length. Knot after 3cm (1⅛in)
adjusting as necessary to fit.
Trim off the excess threads.

CRYSTAL HEART EARRINGS
by Dorothy Wood

You Will Need:

14mm blue heart beads
Czech Crystal

◆

6mm and 4mm bicone beads
Czech Crystal

◆

Jump rings

◆

Headpins

◆

Silver-plated chain

◆

Two earring wires

1. Cut a 4cm (1½in) length of chain. Attach a crystal heart to the bottom of the chain with a jump ring.

2. Pick up a 6mm bicone crystal on a headpin. Bend the headpin over at right angles and trim to 7mm (⁹⁄₃₂in). Use round-nose pliers to bend the headpin round to form a small loop.

3. Repeat to make two dangles with 6mm bicones. Open the loops one at a time and attach each of the bicone dangles to a 2cm–3cm (¾in–1⅛in) length of chain.

4. Cut one headpin to 2.5cm (1in), thread on a 4mm bicone and make a loop at the top. Repeat with a 3.5cm (1⅜in) long headpin.

5. Open a large jump ring and add the heart chain. Pick up the small bicone dangles, one on each side, then the remaining chains so that the bicones are staggered. Close the jump ring. Open the loop on an earring wire and attach the jump ring. Make a second earring to match.

BEAUTIFUL BLUE BRACELET
by Alison Myer

You Will Need:

22-26 8mm glass faceted
aquamarine beads

◆

Three metal beads

◆

Elastic nylon thread

◆

6mm silver jump ring

◆

Three silver headpins

1. Cut a piece of elastic nylon thread measuring approximately 30cm (12in). For a medium bracelet thread on 24 8mm beads (small 22, large 26).

2. Take the ends of the elastic and tie a knot pulling tight to draw each end of the bead string together. Tie two or three more knots, pulling very tight each time so the knot does not unravel (don't worry, the elastic shouldn't snap). Snip the ends of the elastic of neatly next to the knot.

3. Thread each metal bead onto a headpin. Using round-nose pliers, twist the top of the wire to form a loop and snip with wire cutters to form a closed circle. Further close up the loop using pliers if necessary: there should be no gap to ensure the bead does not fall off the jump ring.

4. Take each one of the metal bead charms and thread carefully onto a single jump ring. Then thread the jump ring onto the bead bracelet and close.

BEADING

BEADED SCARF
by Laura Whitcher

You Will Need:

4mm (US size 6)
knitting needles

◆

Cable needle

◆

3 x 50g balls blue yarn
Patons Diploma Gold DK
Pastel Blue (06306)

◆

Three blue mini
daisy bead packs
Craft Time

◆

Blue sewing thread
Gutermann colour 75

1. Knit the beaded scarf following the pattern below:

Using 4mm knitting needles and blue yarn, cast on 50 stitches.
Row 1: (WS) Knit.
Row 2: (RS) Purl 22sts, slip 2sts onto cable needle, leave at back, k1, k2 from cable needle, slip 1 stitch onto cable needle, leave at front, k2, knit stitch from cable needle, p22.
Row 3: K22sts, p1, add bead (by slipping onto the stitch using a sewing needle and blue thread), p2, add bead, p1, k22.

Row 4: P22, k6, p22.
Row 5: K22 sts, p1, add bead, p2, add bead, p1, k22
Row 6: P22, k6, p22.
Row 7: K22, p6, k22.
Repeat Rows 2–7, placing the beads in a line as you go. Continue in this way, leaving approximately 80cm (32in) for casting off.

2. To finish neatly stitch the ends into the back of the cast on/off rows. With wrong side facing, pin out the knitted scarf using glass headed pins to the correct size. Cover with a damp cloth and press gently using a steam iron.

MONOCHROME NECKLACE
by Dorothy Wood

You Will Need:

Black and white beads
The Bead Café

◆

Leather thong

◆

Silver spring ring

◆

Silver headpins

◆

Two thong ends

1. Sort the beads to find the larger beads for the bottom dangles of the necklace. To make the first dangle, thread a seed bead then one or two large beads onto a headpin leaving at least 7mm (⁹⁄₃₂in) of headpin at the top. Trim headpin to 7mm (⁹⁄₃₂in) and make a loop with round-nose pliers.

2. Make a second dangle using one of the larger crystals. Thread both dangles onto a length of leather thong and drop down to the middle.

3. Make two smaller dangles, one crystal, one opaque. If the headpin pulls through the larger bead holes, pick up a seed bead first. Thread the two dangles onto the thong and tie an overhand knot. Make two more dangles and tie in a knot to the other side of the thong, positioning the knot about 2.5cm (1in) higher than on the other side.

4. Continue to add dangles to another five knots spaced every 5cm (2in) or so.

5. Once you are happy with the length of the necklace, trim the thong. Attach a thong end to each end using flat-nose pliers. Open the silver spring ring and attach to the right side of the necklace.

BEADING

BEADED BRAID BRACELET
by Verity Graves-Morris

You Will Need:

Pastel seed bead pack

◆

Three shades of
stranded cotton (floss)
Assorted DMC colours

◆

Safety pins

1. Pick three colours. Take the first colour thread and cut it so that the length is the distance from your fingertip to your shoulder. Repeat this until you have six pieces of stranded cotton in total – two pieces per colour. Then tie one big knot with all the threads.

2. To hold the bracelet in place while you're making it, put a safety pin through the knotted end and pin it to a cushion.

3. Take the far left thread and make a forward knot. The first thread on the left is always the primary. Repeat this knot on the same thread, then discard the second thread to the left. Take the primary thread and repeat the double knot on the third thread, and so on.

4. Start the next row using the thread to the far left. This now becomes your primary thread. Repeat all the steps until you have the row done.

5. Once you've produced some rows, thread a needle through the first thread. Thread the needle through a seed bead, and pull it up tight to the rows. You could thread the stranded cotton directly through the seed bead if it is easier. Put up to four beads on the thread, then secure with a single knot. Repeat this with each piece of thread.

6. Continue knotting the thread (as in step 3), breaking it up intermittently with a few rows of beads. Keep going until the bracelet is long enough to fit around your wrist comfortably To make that sure it fits well, try it on your wrist – there should be enough for you to fit two fingers in next to your wrist, since the bracelet can shrink in water and become too tight (although it will stretch back out when dry).

CAKE DECORATING

BEAUTIFUL BIRDIE BISCUITS
by Ruth Clemens

You Will Need:

Circular biscuits
(7.5cm/3in diameter)

◆

White, blue, purple
and pink sugarpaste

◆

Pink, purple, golden yellow
and black royal icing

◆

Fluted cookie cutter and
small round cutter

◆

Petal cutters
Large, small and extra
small rose petal

1. Roll out the white sugarpaste to 3mm (⅛in) thick; cut out a fluted circle. Secure to the top of a biscuit using a little water.

2. Roll out the blue sugarpaste to 2mm (³⁄₃₂in) thick; cut out the bird's body using the large petal cutter and use the small round cutter to cut out the bird's head. Roll out the purple sugarpaste to 2mm (³⁄₃₂in) thick and cut out three tail feathers with the extra small petal cutter. Set aside.

3. Roll out the pink sugarpaste, to 2mm (³⁄₃₂in) thick and cut out a small petal for the bird's wing. Pinch the thin end of the petal and curve the shape slightly to create the curve of the wing. Use a knife to mark three lines along the wing.

4. Start to build the bird onto the biscuit using the pieces you have cut out. Start with the tail feathers securing them in position with a dab of water. Add the body, the head and finally the wing.

5. Using the black royal icing, pipe a dot for the bird's eye and two legs. Add a beak with golden yellow royal icing.

6. Finally pipe three pink bulbs between the bird's feet and tail feathers and three purple bulbs to the right of the bird's head.

CAKE DECORATING

LITTLE POT CUPCAKES
by Zoe Scott

You Will Need:

Cake mixture

◆

Six-cup king size muffin tin

◆

Lily and leaf cutter set

◆

Silver edible lustre spray

◆

Buttercream

◆

White, yellow and
green sugarpaste

◆

Grey food colouring

1. Grease, then line the muffin tin with 12 strips of greaseproof paper 20cm (7⅞in) long arranged in crosses in each hole of the tin. Pour in the cake mixture and bake until it springs back to the touch. Allow to cool slightly, then use the paper to remove. Once the muffins have cooled, set one aside; spread buttercream over the other five, covering all the sides, using a palette knife to smooth the surface.

2. Take 500g (2lb 2oz) of sugarpaste, colour grey and roll out on a surface dusted with icing sugar. Cut strips approximately 30cm x 10cm (11⅞in x 3⅞in) wide and wrap around the muffin smoothing as you go. Use the base of the muffin tin to cut circles of grey for the pot base and 2cm (¾in) wide strips to wrap around for the rim of the pot. Spray the 'pots' all over with the silver lustre spray. Allow to dry.

3. Using the set aside muffin, crumble and sprinkle over the top of the pots for 'soil'.

4. Using the lily cutter and former, cut petals from rolled out yellow sugarpaste and gently press into place to make the flowers. Use the leaf cutters to make leaves from green sugarpaste. Place the flowers and leaves on the 'soil'.

CAKE DECORATING

SUPERSTAR CAKE POPS

by James Brooks

You Will Need:

Cake

◆

Dark cooking chocolate

◆

Buttercream

◆

15cm (6in) lollipop sticks

◆

Star plunger cutters

◆

Sugarpaste

◆

Gold edible lustre spray

1. Crumble the cake into a mixing bowl. Bind your cake crumb with buttercream at a ratio of 2:1 – two parts cake to one part binding.

2. Roll your mixture into balls of roughly 3cm–4cm (1⅛in–1½in) diameter (approximately 25g/1oz), put them on a sheet of baking paper on a tray, and place them in your freezer for 15 minutes, or your refrigerator for an hour or so, to firm up.

3. Use a lollipop stick to poke a hole half way into each ball. Pour a little melted chocolate into each hole and then insert your sticks. Freeze or refrigerate the cake pops again to harden the chocolate, which helps keep the sticks in place.

4. Get a big bowl full of melted chocolate and dip each cake pop in until fully coated. Shake off the excess chocolate and then place your cake pops in a cake pop stand.

5. Finally, roll out 1mm–2mm (³⁄₃₂in) thick sheets of sugarpaste and make some stars using your star plunger cutters; spray them gold with the lustre spray. Allow to dry and then attach them to your pops using a dab of chocolate and place in the refrigerator to dry. Drizzle your cake pops with melted white chocolate for added indulgence!

CAKE DECORATING

ELEGANT MINI CAKES
by Ruth Clemens

You Will Need:

6.5cm (2½in) mini cakes

◆

Buttercream

◆

10cm (4in) cake card

◆

Purple sugarpaste

◆

White sugar florist
paste (SFP)

◆

Purple royal icing

◆

No.2 piping nozzle

◆

Flower cutters
Large, medium and small carnation

◆

Edible glue

◆

Ball tool and flower pad

◆

Purple edible lustre dust

◆

White holographic
cake sparkles

◆

Purple ribbon

1. Roll out purple sugarpaste to 2mm–3mm (³⁄₃₂in–⅛in) thick to cover the cake card; secure in place using a light mist of water. Set aside.

2. Prepare your mini cake for covering by coating with a thin layer of buttercream.

3. Roll out the purple sugarpaste this time to a depth of 5mm (³⁄₁₆in) on a surface lightly dusted with icing sugar to prevent it from sticking. Use to cover your mini cake smoothing to a fine finish using a cake smoother. Position each cake in the centre of a covered cake card securing it with a dot of buttercream.

4. Roll out the white SFP very thinly to a 1mm–2mm (³⁄₃₂in) thickness. Cut out one large, four medium and four small carnations. Set them onto the flower pad and use the ball tool to thin the edges of the petals, pressing them in a circular motion.

5. Using the recesses of an empty egg tray create the three flowers for the cake. Beginning with the largest flower lay the following together securing each layer with a dab of edible glue:
Large flower: one large, two medium and one small.
Medium flower: two medium and one small.
Small flower: two small. Allow to dry.

6. Fill a piping bag fitted with a no.2 nozzle with purple royal icing. Beginning at the base of the cake pipe swirly lines all over until the cake is completely covered. Set aside to dry.

7. Using the purple lustre dust with a dry paintbrush, dust the centres of the three flowers to create a subtle hint of colour.

8. Once the flowers have dried, position them onto the cake securing with a bulb of royal icing. Pipe small dots of purple royal icing to create the flower centres. Sprinkle on some white holographic cake sparkles for a touch of glitz! Trim the cake base with a purple ribbon.

CAKE DECORATING

PANSY POSY CUPCAKES

by Prudence Rogers

You Will Need:

Vanilla cupcakes baked in
cupcake liners
Cath Kidston Green Polka Dot

◆

Vanilla buttercream

◆

Sugarpaste

◆

White royal icing

◆

Pansy flower and leaf cutters

◆

Edible black pen

◆

Red, orange and light
green gel food colouring

1. Colour three small amounts of sugarpaste dark pink, orange and light green using the gel food colourings.

2. Roll out the dark pink and orange sugarpaste to 2mm (³⁄₃₂in) thick and use a pansy cutter to cut petals. Join four petals together using a little water to create a flower. Place into an empty egg box to create a cupped shape and leave to dry. Make four or five flowers for each cupcake.

3. Roll out the light green sugarpaste to 2mm (³⁄₃₂in) thick. Cut out eight or nine leaves for each cupcake using the leaf cutter. Use a blunt knife pressed lightly into the surface of the leaves to create the veins. Leave to dry.

4. Take thevanilla cupcakes baked in cupcake liners and, when cooled, pipe with a swirl of vanilla buttercream. Use white royal icing to pipe a small curved centre onto each flower.

5. Then use an edible black pen to create lines radiating from the middle. Stick your pansies onto the buttercream, alternating between pink and orange flowers. Leave small gaps between groups of flowers and intersperse with the leaves.

CAKE DECORATING

CHRISTMAS TREE CAKES
by Zoe Scott

You Will Need:

Fruit cake mixture

♦

Six-cup king size muffin tin

♦

Red, green and gold
cake glitter
Holly Cupcake

♦

Apricot jam and marzipan

♦

Homemade royal icing
(see step 3)

1. Grease the six-cup king size muffin tin, cut 12 strips of greaseproof paper 20cm (7⅞in) long, arrange in crosses in each hole of the tin. Pour in the fruit cake mixture and bake in a bain marie, until a skewer comes out clean; cool slightly then use the paper to remove.

2. Once cool, brush cakes with apricot jam, roll out the marzipan and cut four circles approximately 22cm (8⅝in) in diameter (use a side plate as a guide). Cut approximately a third out of each circle to make a cone of marzipan around the cakes, using the cut outs for the remaining two cakes.

3. Make the royal icing. Whisk three egg whites to soft peaks then gradually add 550g (2lb 4oz) icing sugar until stiff peaks form. Finally add a teaspoon of glycerine with some green food colouring. Using a small palette knife spread the icing over the cakes. Starting at the base dab and pull the palette knife to create peaks.

4. From the remaining marzipan cut six stars and roll lots of small balls for baubles.

5. Brush with jam, then sprinkle with the gold cake glitter. Sprinkle the trees with green cake glitter and then decorate with the stars and baubles.

6. For an extra touch, cut squares of cake and cover with marzipan and royal icing coloured with red and sprinkle with the red cake glitter to make presents for the bottom of the trees. Leave the finished cakes to dry overnight or up to two days, until firm.

CAKE DECORATING

PINK DAISY CUPCAKES
by Ruth Clemens

You Will Need:

Six cupcakes baked in
white paper cases

◆

Buttercream

◆

Circular cookie cutter

◆

Sage, pink and pale
pink sugarpaste

◆

White royal icing

◆

No.2 piping nozzle

◆

Flower cutters
Large and small daisy plunger
cutters and medium calyx cutter

1. Roll out the sage sugarpaste
to 3mm (⅛in) thick and cut out round
circles to fit the cupcake tops.

2. Coat the tops of the
cupcakes with a thin layer of
buttercream and place the sage
green circles in position.

3. Add the white royal icing
to a piping bag fitted with a no.2
piping nozzle. From the centre pipe
four lines right up to the edge of
the case, dividing the cupcake
into quarters. Between each full
length line pipe a shorter line
to reach half way between the
centre and the outside edge.

CAKE DECORATING

4. Now pipe a line between each full length and half length lines that reaches approximately three-quarters of the way to the outside edge. Pipe two dots following each short line. Finish all of the other piped lines with a bulb at the end of each. If your royal icing dots have peaks, dab them down gently with a damp paintbrush. Set the cupcakes aside to dry.

5. Roll out the pink sugarpaste paste to a thickness of 2mm (³⁄₃₂in) on a surface lightly dusted with icing sugar to prevent it from sticking. Cut out six large daisies. Repeat with the pale pink sugarpaste cutting out six small daisies. Cut out six medium calyx from the sage green sugarpaste.

6. Apply a dot of royal icing to the centre of the cupcake and place the calyx in position. Add another dot of royal icing to the centre of the calyx and add the large pink daisy. The small pale pink daisy is secured in the centre using a small dab of water applied to the back. Pipe small dots of royal icing to create the centres of the flowers using a damp paintbrush to flatten any peaks.

CAKE DECORATING

CELEBRATION MINI CAKES

by Sue Ellis

You Will Need:

Cake ingredients and brandy

◆

Apricot jam and marzipan

◆

Six 7.5cm (3in) diameter baking tins

◆

Cutters in a variety of shapes

◆

Mini cake boards

◆

White ready-roll fondant icing

◆

Ribbon

1. Make a fruit cake mix using the ingredients for a 20cm (8in) Christmas cake recipe. Line the baking tins with greaseproof paper and divide the cake mixture equally between them. Bake until golden brown on a low heat setting 140°C, 275°F, Gas Mark 1. Allow to cool.

2. Douse the cakes in brandy and leave them to mature. Two weeks before event, place each on a mini cake board, coat with warm apricot jam and cover with marzipan.

3. When you are ready to cover your cakes with the fondant icing, you will need to prepare them by brushing them lightly with boiled water so that the icing adheres to the marzipan.

4. Roll out the fondant icing to about 2mm (³⁄₃₂in) thick, lay it on top of the cake and use a smoother to gently smooth over the top and down around the sides. Trim off the excess icing and repeat until all cakes are covered and smooth.

5. Decorate the top of each cake with your own sugar decorations made from fondant icing. Use hearts and moulded flowers for Valentines day or weddings. Create stars for birthdays and for a festive Christmas theme use snowflake or holly cutters. All icing can be coloured using edible paste or dust and to add a sparkle, lustre dust can be used to brush gently on top. Just add ribbon to the cake base complete the right look for the occasion.

CAKE DECORATING

FRILLY FLOWER CUPCAKES
by Fiona Rinaldi

You Will Need:

Cupcakes baked in black polka dot cupcake cases

◆

Garrett frill cutter set

◆

White flower paste

◆

Buttercream and pink sugarpaste

◆

Edible glue

◆

Decorative edge punch
Martha Stewart doily lace

◆

A4 silver paper

1. Roll out some flower paste finely with a non-stick rolling pin. Use a garret frill cutter to cut out four ring-shaped pieces with scalloped edges. Roll a cocktail stick (toothpick) backwards and forwards on the scalloped edges to frill them. Cut each ring with a knife so that the frill can be opened out into a strip.

2. Arrange the first frilled strip into a circle, making sure the diameter of the circle is slightly smaller than the top of the cupcake.

3. Using a thin paintbrush, add a small amount of edible glue to the non-frilled edge of the circle and attach the next frilled strip in a circular motion. Continue this process until all frilled strips have been added and the hole in the centre of the circle is completely filled. You will need four frilly strips for each flower.

4. Use pieces of kitchen towel or a paper napkin to separate the frilly layers while they are drying.

5. Decorate the tops of your cakes with circles of pink sugarpaste. Once the flowers have dried, transfer each onto the top of a cupcake and attach with buttercream.

6. To make a cupcake wrapper, use scissors to cut a silver paper arc long enough to wrap around the cake. Use the edge punch along the longer side of the paper arc for a lace pattern. Wrap around the cupcake with the lace pattern at the top and secure with double-sided tape.

CAKE DECORATING

MINI CHRISTMAS PUDDING CAKES

by Zoe Scott

You Will Need:

Fruit cake mixture

◆

Six-cup king size muffin tin

◆

Holly cutter

◆

Red, gold and green
cake glitter
Holly Cupcake

◆

Homemade fondant icing

◆

Green and red sugarpaste

1. Grease the muffin tin, cut 12 strips of greaseproof paper 20cm (7⅞in) long, arrange in crosses in each hole of the tin. Pour in the fruit cake mixture and bake in a bain marie until a skewer comes out clean; cool slightly then use the paper to remove.

2. Roll out the green sugarpaste and cut out 12 holly leaves. Moisten slightly with a drop of water and sprinkle with green cake glitter.

3. Roll 18 balls of red sugarpaste, moisten slightly and sprinkle with red cake glitter.

4. Mix up fondant icing and dip each cake narrow end in up to half way and quickly turn back onto the wider base to allow the fondant to drip; sprinkle with gold cake glitter.

5. Add the holly leaves and berries on top of the fondant icing whilst still wet and leave to firm, then store in an airtight container until serving.

CAKE DECORATING

BUTTON BLOSSOM CUPCAKES
by Ruth Clemens

You Will Need:

Six cupcakes baked in white paper cases

◆

Buttercream

◆

Circular cookie cutter

◆

Purple and lime green sugarpaste

◆

Purple royal icing

◆

No.2 piping nozzle

◆

Flower cutters
Small five-petal blossom cutter and small blossom plunger cutter

1. Roll out the lime green sugarpaste to 2mm (3/32in) thick on a surface lightly dusted with icing sugar. Cut out six small five-petal blossoms and 24 small blossoms with the plunger cutter. Place the five-petal blossoms into the recesses of an empty egg box to help shape the petals. To create the buttons for the centres of the five-petal blossoms, roll out a little purple sugarpaste to 3mm (⅛in) thick.

2. Using the wide end of the no.2 piping nozzle cut out 6 circles. Make two indents in each button for the centre. Apply a dab of water to the centre of each blossom and place a button, securing with a light press.

3. Coat the tops of the cupcakes with a thin layer of buttercream and place on purple circles cut to fit from purple sugarpaste rolled out to 3mm (⅛in) thick.

4. Add the purple royal icing to a piping bag fitted with the no.2 nozzle. Secure the large blossom in position on the top of the cupcake using a dot of royal icing. Position the small blossoms across the tops of the cupcakes adhering with a little water applied to the back of each. Pipe small dots to the centre of each small blossom and then pipe small bulbs of royal icing for the polka dots, dabbing down any peaks with a damp paintbrush.

CAKE DECORATING

CROCHET

PATCH CUSHION
by Kirsty Neale

You Will Need:

4mm (US size G/6) crochet hook

◆

1 x 50g ball green yarn
1 x 50g ball cream yarn
1 x 50g ball lime yarn
Rowan Cotton Glace Ivy (812),
Rowan Cashsoft DK Cream (500) and
Rowan Cashsoft DK Lime (509)

◆

Fabric for cushion front:
Four pieces 22cm x 22cm
(8⅝in x 8⅝in)
Dena Fishbein Kumari Garden Teja
Pink, Tanya Whelan Delilah Amelie
White, Amy Butler Soul Blossoms
Buttercups Spearmint and Amy Butler
Soul Blossoms Passion Lily Cerise Pink

Fabric for cushion back:
Two pieces 40cm x 23cm
(15½in x 9in)
Tilda Christmas House Big Spot Pink

1. To make the cushion front, sew two of the fabric squares together along one edge; repeat for the other two fabric squares. Press the seams flat. Lining up the centre joins, stitch the two pairs together to make a four-square patch.

2. Crochet a green and cream granny square measuring approximately 15cm (6in).

3. Pin the crochet square to the middle of the fabric patch and sew in place. Add lines of running stitch between the corners of the crochet and the fabric.

4. To make an envelope back, first fold over and stitch a narrow double hem down one long edge of each cushion back piece.

5. With right sides facing, pin the hemmed rectangles to the cushion front with the hemmed edges overlapping in the centre. Stich around all four sides of the square.

6. Trim the excess fabric across the cushion corners, remove the pins, and turn the right way out. Press all seams for a neat finish, and insert a cushion pad to fit.

BABY BLANKET
by Lynda Wainwright

You Will Need:

4mm (US size G/6)
crochet hook

◆

4 x 50g balls purple yarn **(MC)**
2 x 50g balls white yarn **(C)**
Patons Fairytale DK Hollyhock
(06373) and Vanilla (06302)

or

5 x 50g balls red spotted yarn
Patons Fairytale DK Red Spot (06380)

1. First work a tension square:
8 rows and 16 sts to 10cm (3⅞in)
worked in pattern.

2. You must decide whether you
will be working the single colour
blanket or the striped blanket,
and crochet your chosen desing
following the pattern below:

Foundation rows
Make 82ch.
Work 1tr into 3rd ch from hook, (1tr
in each chain) to end, turn. (80sts)

Pattern rows
This is a 2 row pattern.
Row 1: Make 1ch, 1dc in between
1st 2tr of last row, *3ch, miss
next 3tr, 1dc in between last of
the 3 missed tr and next tr, 1ch,
miss next tr, 1 dc in between next

trs as before, repeat from * to
last st, ending last rep after 3ch,
work 1dc into top of last st, turn.
Row 2: 3ch, *work 3tr into 3ch
space, miss next dc, 1tr into
next 1ch sp, miss next dc, rep
from * ending last rep at 3tr
in 3ch sp, 1ddc into last st.
Repeat pattern rows 1 and 2.
For single colour blanket:
Continue the 2 pattern rows until 90
pattern rows have been worked.
For striped blanket: Work 4
rows in MC followed by 2 rows in
C. Continue until 90 pattern rows
have been worked. Fasten off.

Shell edging
(If using 2 colours join C to the top
right corner, work 1dc all around the
body of the blanket working 3dc into
each corner and complete in MC.)
Join yarn to the 2nd dc from any
corner of the blanket, work 1ch,
(miss 1st dc, 5tr into next dc, miss
1dc, 1dc into next dc), repeat around
the edge working the 'shell' into
the middle st of each corner, sl
st into beginning ch. Fasten off.

3. Sew in all ends, and block and
press as detailed on the yarn band.

CROCHET

FLOWER COASTERS
by Grace Harvey

You Will Need:

3mm (US size C/2)
crochet hook

◆

1 x 100g ball turquoise yarn
1 x 100g ball lime yarn
1 x 100g ball green yarn
Patons 100% Cotton 4 Ply Jade (01726),
Apple (01205) and Green (01727)

1. Make a coaster following the crochet pattern below:

Foundation ring: Make 7ch, sl st into 1st ch to form ring.
Rnd 1: 2ch (counts as 1st tr), 2ch, *1tr into ring, 2ch, rep from * 8 more times, sl st into 3rd ch at beg of round. (10 spokes coming out of ring)
Rnd 2: Sl st into 1st 2ch sp from prev round, 3ch (counts as 1tr), work 2tr into same ch sp as sl st, 1ch, miss next tr, *3tr into next ch sp, 1ch, rep from * until all ch sp have been worked into, sl st into 3rd ch at beg of round. (10 sections of 3)
Rnd 3: *4tr, then 1ch. Repeat from * 9 times. Sl st through the 1st tr to complete the circle.
Rnd 4: Sl st into 1st 1ch sp from prev round, 4ch (counts as 1tr & 1ch), *miss 4tr, 5tr into next 1ch sp, 1ch, rep from * 8 more times, 4tr into last 1ch space sl st into 3rd of 4ch at beg of round. (10 sections of 4)
Rnd 5: Sl st into 1st 1ch sp from prev round, 4ch (counts as 1tr and 1ch), *miss 5tr, 7tr into next 1ch sp, 1ch, rep from * 8 more times, 6tr into last 1ch space sl st into 3rd of 4ch at beg of round. (10 sections of 7)

2. Break off yarn and sew in loose ends. Pin out on ironing board and cover with damp cloth, press with steam iron.

RUSTLING BABY BALL
by Fiona-Grace Peppler

You Will Need:

4mm (US size G/6)
crochet hook

◆

1 x 50g ball blue yarn **(MC)**
1 x 50g ball grey yarn **(C)**
Rowan Purelife Revive
Grit (473) and Pumice (476)

◆

Toy filling

◆

Two drink bottle caps and
two buttons (for rattle)

◆

Recycled plastic bag and
scrap of light cotton

1. Make 12 pentagon pieces, following the pattern below:

Foundation ring: 4ch in yarn C – join with sl st to form ring.
Rnd 1: 3ch (counts as 1tr), 9tr into ring, join with sl st to 3rd ch. (10 sts) Break off yarn C and join in MC.
Rnd 2: 1ch, *3dc into next st, 1dc into next st, rep from * 4 more times, join with sl st into 1ch at beg of round. (20sts)
Rnd 3: 1ch, *3dc into next st, 1dc into next 3dc, rep from * 4 more times, join with sl st into 1ch at beg of round. (30sts)

Rnd 4: 1ch, *3dc into next st, 1dc into next 5dc, rep from * 4 more times, join with sl st into 1ch at beg of round. (40sts)
Rnd 5: 1ch, *3dc into next st, 1dc into next 7dc, rep from * 4 more times, join with sl st into 1ch at beg of round. (50sts)

2. Assemble the pentagons into a ball using double crochet and yarn C, so each piece is surrounded by five others. Leave a gap to allow for stuffing (three sides open).

3. Cut the corner from an old plastic bag and use it to line the ball. Half stuff firmly with toy filling.

4. To make the rattle, tape the bottle caps together, having put two small buttons loose inside the cavity first. For the sake of safety, stitch the rattle inside a scrap of cloth, before placing in the ball. Stuff firmly around it. Sew the edges of the plastic bag together. Crochet the remaining edges closed.

CROCHET

REVERSIBLE HEADSCARF

by Kirsty Neale

You Will Need:

3mm (US size C/2)
crochet hook

◆

1 x 50g ball yarn
Rowan Wool Cotton Elf (green 946)

or

Rowan Cashsoft DK Sweet (lilac 501)

◆

Two triangles of contrasting
fabric 34cm (13½in) wide x
22cm (8⅝in) high
Amy Butler Soul Blossoms Passion
Lily Cerise Pink and Dena Fishbein
Kumari Garden Tanaya Pink

or

Dena Fishbein Kumari Garden
Sujata Blue and Tarika Moss

1. The fabric size can be adjusted if you prefer to make a bigger or smaller headscarf. Fold over and press a 1.5cm (⅝in) hem along the top edge of each of the fabric triangles.

2. With right sides facing, pin and stitch together along the two sloping sides. Snip off the point, turn the right way out and press along the seams.

3. Sew the top edges together with blanket stitch using your chosen yarn colour (if it's too chunky, separate the yarn into strands and just use half the thickness).

4. Crochet a chain 30cm–40cm (12in–15½in) long. Then work a double crochet through the top of the first and every following blanket stitch running along the top of your fabric triangle.

5. Continue crocheting to form another chain 30cm–40cm (12in–15½in) long, to end up with a chain-stitched ties at either side of the finished headscarf.

CROCHET

BABY BUGGY CHUNKY RUG
by Lisa Fordham

You Will Need:

5mm (US size H/8)
crochet hook

◆

3 x 100g balls white yarn
2 x 100g balls green yarn
2 x 100g balls blue yarn
Rowan Cocoon Polar (801),
Kiwi (816) and Seascape (813)

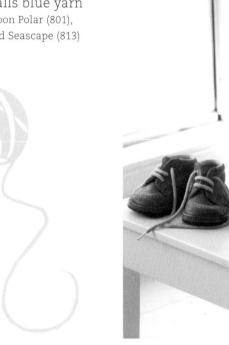

1. You will need 12 granny squares made from three contrasting yarn colours. You can make your squares using any pattern to achieve different finishes. Make four of each colour, each measuring approximately 25cm x 25cm (10in x 10in).

2. When all 12 granny squares are complete, lay them out to form an attractive pattern in rows of three squares across by four squares down.

3. Using safety pins, pin together the granny squares from the front.

4. Using dc stitch throughout, crochet the squares together to form strips, then crochet the strips together to form the rug. Finish off by crocheting around the outer edge – working 3sts into the corners.

GRANNY SQUARE SLIPPERS

by Fiona-Grace Peppler

You Will Need:

3.5mm (US size E/4)
crochet hook

◆

1 x 50g ball blue yarn **(MC)**
1 x 50g ball pink yarn **(C)**
Patons Dreamtime 3 Ply Pastel Blue
(02934) and Sweet Pink (00333)

◆

Dog and cat iron-on motifs

◆

Four pink or blue buttons

1. Measure the length of the baby's foot. Divide this measurement in half to give you the diagonal width required for each granny square.

2. Make six crochet squares for each slipper, following the pattern below, starting with MC yarn and completing the final round in C yarn. Two squares laid corner to corner should be as long as baby's foot.

Foundation ring: 4ch, join with sl st to form a ring.
Rnd 1: 1ch, 12dc into ring, join with sl st into 1st ch. (12sts)
Rnd 2: 1ch, 1dc into next dc, *3dc into next dc, 1dc into next 2dc, repeat from * twice, 3dc into next dc, 1dc into last dc, join with sl st into 1st ch. (20sts)
Rnd 3: 1ch, 1dc into next 2dc, *3dc into next dc, 1dc into next 4dc, rep from * twice, 3dc into next dc, 1dc into next 2dc, join with sl st into 1st ch. (28sts)
Rnd 4: 1ch, 1 dc into next 3dc, *3dc into next dc, 1dc into next 6dc, repeat from * twice, 3dc into next dc, 1dc into last 3dc, join with sl st into 1st ch. (28sts)
Keeping pattern correct, work as given until required size is achieved, increasing by working 3dc at each corner, working last round in yarn C.

3. Using a blunt needle and a length of yarn, slip stitch four squares together to form the sole and sides. Slip stitch another square to close up one end by folding the sides in to form the toe. Slip stitch two sides of another square to the opposite end to form the heel.

4. Iron the motifs onto the front of the slippers and reinforce with a few stitches.

5. Securely fasten a button at each side of each corner at the back of the slipper.

RIBBED CUSHION COVER
by Lynda Wainwright

You Will Need:

5mm (US size H/8)
crochet hook

◆

3 x 100g balls crimson yarn
Patons Wool Blend Aran Berry (00136)

or

2 x 100g balls beige yarn
2 x 100g balls purple yarn
Patons Wool Blend Aran
Beige (00011) and Purple (00149)

1. First work a tension square: 15 sts and 12 rows to 10cm (3⅞in) worked in pattern; adjust hook size if necessary.

2. Using the yarn colour of your choice, make a crochet square following the pattern below:

Foundation row: (RS) Work 1dc into 2nd ch from hook, 1dc into each ch to end. (30sts)
Row 1: 2ch, 1tr around stem of each of the next 29dc, by inserting hook from right to left around the stem and completing stitch as normal, 1htr into top of turning ch.
Row 2: 1ch, 1dc in each of next 29tr, 1dc in 2nd turning ch. Rows 2 and 3 form the pattern. Work 20 more rows. Fasten off.

3. Work seven more squares. If using two colours, make four in each colour. Weave in ends and block to measure 20cm (7⅞in) square.

4. For the cushion front lay out four squares so the rib alternates.

5. Pick up two squares with wrong sides facing and join together with a row of double crochet. Repeat with the remaining two squares. Join the two strips of two squares, wrong sides facing, with a row of double crochet. Repeat for the cushion back.

6. Weave in all loose ends. Place the front and back with wrong sides facing and join together along three sides with a row of double crochet. Insert a cushion pad and close. Fasten off yarn.

POMPOM GARLAND

by Kirsty Neale

You Will Need:

3mm (US size C/2)
crochet hook

◆

1 x 50g ball cream yarn
1 x 50g ball blue yarn
1 x 50g ball lime yarn
1 x 50g ball red yarn
1 x 50g ball lilac yarn
1 x 50g ball grey yarn

Rowan Cashsoft DK Cream (500),
Kingfisher (525), Lime (509), Poppy
(512), Sweet (501) and Tape (515)

◆

Pompom maker
Milward pompom set

◆

Assorted bright ribbons

1. Wrap yarn in the first of your chosen colours around a pompom maker. Snip the strands around the edges, and then tie a length of thread around the middle to hold the finished pompom together. Make more in different sizes, using a variety of yarn colours.

2. Crochet a chain for the garland string. Thread the chain onto a large needle, and push it gently through the centre of the first pompom, and slide it along.

3. Add more pompoms in the same way. Position along the length of the chain spacing them as evenly as you like.

4. To create individual hanging decorations, take one pompom; thread a length of yarn onto a large needle and, holding one end, push it down through the pompom, bringing it back up a short distance away. Slip the needle off, and knot the yarn ends together.

5. Pull gently on the looped end to form a hanger for your decoration. Tie a ribbon bow around the hanger, so it sits right on top of the pompom.

CROCHET

CROSS STITCH

MINI HOME CUSHION

by Jayne Schofield

You Will Need:

White 14-count aida

◆

Pink, light pink, yellow, lime, jade, fawn and lilac stranded cotton (floss)
DMC colours 3805, 3608, 727, 3819, 959, Ecru and 340

◆

Toy filling

◆

Two pieces of pink felt 16.5cm (6½in) square

1. Cross stitch the design onto aida following the chart, using two strands of stranded cotton throughout. Trim to leave five rows of fabric all the way around the design.

2. Sew the aida to the centre of one of the felt pieces with running stitch worked white thread. Tack (baste) then sew the two pieces of felt together with blanket stitch using two strands of light pink (DMC 3608), leaving a 5cm (2in) gap for stuffing. Fill lightly then continue with blanket stitch to close the gap.

Key:

■ DMC 3805	■ DMC 3608
■ DMC Ecru	■ DMC 959
■ DMC 340	■ DMC 3819
■ DMC 727	

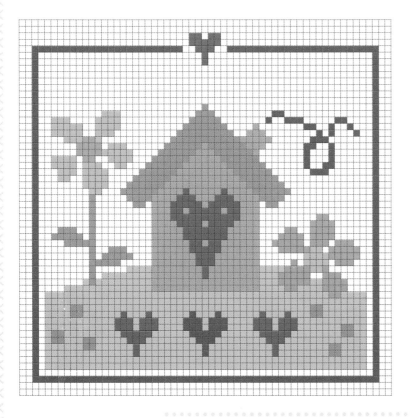

CROSS STITCH

BUNTING BOOKMARK
by Jeni Hennah

You Will Need:

White 14-count aida

◆

Blue, pink, lime, yellow, grey and pale blue stranded cotton (floss)
DMC colours 3845, 601, 906, 726, 844 and 3325

◆

Blue felt

1. Cross stitch the bunting design onto aida with stranded cotton following the chart. Use two strands of blue (DMC 3845), pink (DMC 601), lime green (DMC 906) and yellow (DMC 726) for the flags.

2. Backstitch the 'binding' for the bunting using two strands of dark grey stranded cotton (DMC 844).

3. Cut the aida, allowing 6mm (¼in) all around the bunting design – once cut this should measure approximately 3cm x 15.5cm (1⅛in x 6⅛in).

4. Cut two pieces of blue felt 1cm (⅜in) larger than the aida on all sides – these should be approximately 5cm x 17.5cm (2in x 7in). Attach the aida to the centre of one of the cut pieces of blue felt by sewing with blanket stitch using two strands of pale blue stranded cotton (DMC 3325).

5. Sew the two pieces of blue felt together with blanket stitch using two strands of pale blue stranded cotton (DMC 3325), ensuring that the aida is on the outside.

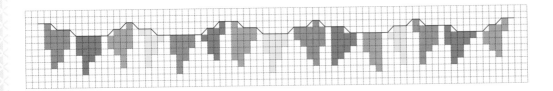

CROSS STITCH

RAINBOW KEYRING

by Grace Harvey

You Will Need:

White 16-count aida

◆

Red, orange, yellow,
green, blue and dark blue
stranded cotton (floss)
DMC colours 666, 741, 743,
907, 3325 and 798

◆

Plastic key ring

1. Disassemble the key ring. Lay the back piece onto the aida and draw around in pencil. Cut out.

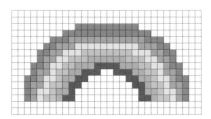

2. Cross stitch the rainbow design centrally onto the aida following the chart. Use two strands of red (DMC 666), orange (DMC741), yellow (DMC743), green (DMC 907), blue (DMC 3325) and dark blue (DMC 798) for the rainbow arcs.

3. Place the aida in the key ring and reassemble.

CROSS STITCH

STRAWBERRY CARD
by Katherine Dyer

You Will Need:

White 14-count aida

◆

Red, dark red, gold, black,
dark green and green
stranded cotton (floss)
DMC colours 349, 321,
729, 310, 319 and 320

◆

Oval aperture card

1. Cut a piece of 14-count aida, ensuring that your fabric will fit to the edge of the card; seal the edges of the aida with masking tape.

2. Cross stitch the strawberry design onto aida with stranded cotton following the chart. Use two strands of dark green (DMC 319) and green (DMC 320) for the stalk, and red (DMC 349) and dark red (DMC 321) for the strawberry.

3. Outline the design using backstitch in one strand of black (DMC 310). Stitch the strawberry pips randomly using backstitch in two strands of gold (DMC 729).

4. Mount the design over the inner aperture of the card with double-sided tape.

CROSS STITCH

ANCHOR BOOK BAG
by Grace Harvey

You Will Need:

White 16-count aida

◆

Dark blue, blue, turquoise,
light blue, red and light red
stranded cotton (floss)
DMC colours 792, 798, 799,
3325, 321 and 963

◆

Fabric for the bag front
and back:
Two pieces 36cm x X38cm
(14½in x 14¾in)
Tilda Red Stripe

◆

Fabric for the lining, handles
and pocket:
Two pieces 36cm x X38cm
(14½in x 14¾in)
Two pieces 10cm x 51cm
(3⅞in x 20⅜in)
One piece 20cm x 20cm
(7⅞in x 7⅞in)
Tea Cakes Petite Fours Cornflower

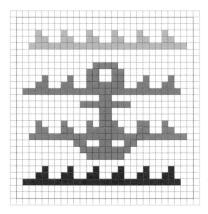

2. Cross stitch the anchor design onto aida with stranded cotton following the chart. Use two strands of light blue (DMC 3325), turquoise (DMC 799), blue (DMC 798) and dark blue (DMC 792) for the waves, red (DMC 321) for the anchor, and light red (DMC 963) for the border. Machine stitch the aida to the centre of the pocket piece.

3. Machine stitch a double hem along the top edge and sides of the pocket, then sew the bottom and sides of the pocket to the bag front.

4. Place the two lining pieces right sides facing; machine stitch along the bottom and sides. Repeat for the two bag pieces. To create the base, pinch the bottom corners of the lining out, flatten and press so that the bottom and side seams align. Machine stitch 2.5cm (1in) in from the corner. Sew the bag front and back together in the same way.

1. Fold both of the handle pieces in half lengthwise, with wrong sides together, and press well. Open out, then fold the outside edges in to meet the centre fold line, wrong sides together, and press. Fold each piece in half again, press once again and then machine stitch along each side.

5. Place the lining inside the bag, right sides facing. Place the handles between the layers of fabric on each side at the top of the bag; pin. Machine stitch around the top of the bag, leaving gap for turning. Turn the bag right sides out and push the lining inside the bag. Machine stitch around the top of the bag.

CROSS STITCH

CUPCAKE CARD
by Jayne Schofield

You Will Need:

White 14-count aida

◆

Pink, light pink,
jade, aqua and lilac
stranded cotton (floss)
DMC colours 3805, 3608,
3819, 959, 3846 and 340

◆

C6 pink card and envelope

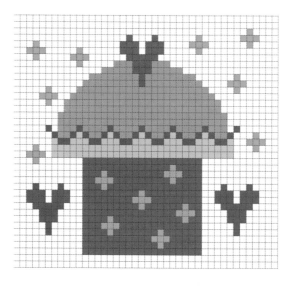

1. Cross stitch the cupcake
design onto aida with stranded
cotton following the chart.
Use two strands of stranded
cotton throughout.

2. Trim leaving four rows
of fabric all the way around the
design. Fray two rows deep around
all the edges. Lightly press.

3. Attach the stitched
cupcake design to the front of
the card using double-sided tape,
being careful to avoid sticking
down the frayed edges.

Key:
- ■ DMC 3805
- ■ DMC Ecru
- ■ DMC 340
- ■ DMC 3608
- ■ DMC 959
- ■ DMC 3819

CROSS STITCH

FLOWER NEEDLE CASE

by Jeni Hennah

You Will Need:

White 28-count linen

◆

Light purple, dark purple,
light green, green and cream
stranded cotton (floss)
DMC colours 340, 3746,
3347, 905 and 745

◆

Purple and blue felt

1. Cross stitch the flower design onto linen with stranded cotton following the chart. Use two strands of light purple (DMC 340) for the flowers and two strands of light green (DMC 3347) for the stems and grass.

2. Backstitch around the edge of the flowers using two strands of dark purple (DMC 3746). Backstitch around the edge of the grass and stems using two strands of dark green (DMC 905).

3. Backstitch the flower centre design using two strands of cream (DMC 745). Cut the linen, allowing 6mm (¼in) all around the flower design – once cut this should measure approximately 5cm x 5cm (2in x 2in).

4. Cut a piece of purple felt measuring 8cm x 16cm (3½in x 6⅜in) and a piece of blue felt measuring 6cm x 14cm (2⅜in x 5½in). Pin the smaller piece to the centre of the larger piece and sew through the middle with backstitch. Fold in half to create a 'book' shape.

5. Attach the linen to the front of the needle case by sewing with blanket stitch using two strands of dark purple (DMC 3746).

6. Take care to ensure that you only sew through the purple felt and not the blue layer of felt inside the needle case.

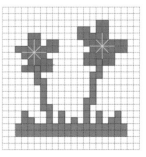

CROSS STITCH

KNITTING

STARRY NIGHT DOORSTOP
by Lisa Fordham

You Will Need:

3.5mm knitting needles

◆

2 x 50g balls black yarn
1 x 25g ball pale yellow yarn
1 x 25g ball silver yarn
Patons Diploma Gold DK Black (06183),
Patons Fab DK Lemon (02330) and
Rowan Shimmer Silver (092)

◆

Black felt

◆

Leftover fabric for inner bag

◆

Clean sand

1. For the inner bag, cut six pieces from your fabric leftovers each measuring 15cm (6in) square. Pin four pieces right sides together in a row; machine stitch. Attach the fifth piece to make the bag bottom. Attach the top panel but leave the last edge unstitched. Turn through. and fill with clean sand; hand stitch the final edge closed.

2. Cast on 25sts and working in garter stitch, knit squares measuring 15cm (6in). Knit four in black and two in pale yellow yarn.

3. Sew the knitted panels together with black yarn, inserting the weighted bag before stitching closed. Cast on 12sts using black yarn and work in garter stitch a 15cm (6in) long strap. Cut a piece of black felt to the same size and sew the two together using a blanket stitch and black yarn.

4. Following the pattern below, knit and attach three stars:

With the pale yellow and silver yarns held together, cast on 55sts. Knit one row.

Next row: K4 sl1, k2tog, psso, *K8, sl1 k2tog, psso; repeat from * to last 4 sts, k4. (45sts)
Next row: K3, sl1, k2tog, psso, *K6, sl1 k2tog, psso; repeat from * to last 3 sts, k3. (35sts)
Next row: K2, sl1, k2tog, psso, *K4, sl1 k2tog, psso; repeat from * to last 2 sts, k2. (25sts)
Next row: K1, sl1, k2tog, psso, *K2, sl1 k2tog, psso; repeat from * to last 2 sts, K1. (15sts)
Next: Sl1, k2tog, psso: repeat from * to end 5sts. Cut yarn, thread through rem sts, draw tight and secure. Sew sides together.

CUTE POCKET DOLL
by Claire Garland

You Will Need:

Four 3.75mm (US size 5) double-pointed needles

◆

1 x 50g ball pink yarn **(MC)**
1 x 100g ball blue yarn **(C)**
1 x 50g ball aqua yarn **(Dress)**
Rowan Pure Wool DK Tudor Rose (046), Patons 100% Cotton 4 Ply Sky (01702) and Patons Diploma Gold DK Aqua (06243)

◆

Toy filling

◆

Pink felt

◆

White sewing thread
Gutermann colour 800

◆

Small safety pin

1. Knit the pocket doll following the pattern below:

Head and body
Using 3.75mm double-pointed needles and MC cast on 10sts.
Step 1: Hold needle with sts in left hand (LH).
Step 2: Hold two empty dpns parallel in right hand.

Step 3: Slip first stitch onto the dpn closest to you and off the LH needle. Slip next stitch onto the dpn furthest away and off the LH needle. Repeat steps 1–3 until all 10sts are divided onto the 2 parallel dpns. Slide sts to other end of dpns. Work in the round over two dpns using a 3rd dpn to knit with.

Rnd 1: Beg with the 5sts at the back, k10.

Rnd 2: (inc) Kf&b, k3, kf&b, kf&b, k3, kf&b. 14sts (7sts on each dpn) Place marker (small safety pin).

Rnd 3: K14.

Rnd 4: (inc) Kf&b, k5, kf&b, kf&b, k5, kf&b. (18sts)

Rnd 5: K18.
Rep Rnd 5 once.

Rnd 7: (inc) Kf&b, k7, kf&b, kf&b, k7, kf&b. (22sts)

Rnd 8: K22.
Rep Rnd 8 once.

Rnd 10: (inc) Kf&b, k9, kf&b, kf&b, k9, kf&b. (26sts)

Rnd 11: K26.
Rep Rnd 11 twice.

Rnd 14: (dec) Sl1, k1, psso, k9, k2tog, sl1, k1, psso, k9, k2tog.

Rnd 15: K22.

Rnd 16: (dec) Sl1, k1, psso, k7, k2tog, sl1, k1, psso, k7, k2tog.

Rnd 17, 19, 21: K.

Rnds 18, 20: decrease 4sts on each rnd; decreasing 1st at beg and end on each dpn. (10sts)
Rep Rnd 21 twice.

Rnd 24: (inc) Kf&b, k3, kf&b, kf&b, k3, kf&b. (14sts)

Rnd 25: K14.

Rnd 26: (inc) Kf&b, k5, kf&b, kf&b, k5, kf&b. (18sts)

Rnd 27: K18.
Rep Rnd 27 16 times.
Stuff the head and the body.

Legs

Rnd 44: (dec) K4, sl1, k1, psso, k3, k4, sl1, k1, psso, k3. (16sts)

Rnd 45: K4, slide next 8sts off needles onto safety pin, k4 from back needle. (8sts)

*Rnd 46: K8.
Rep last rnd until leg, measures 15cm (6in) (K2tog) 4 times. (4sts)
Cut yarn, thread end through sts.**
Rejoin yarn to rem 8sts, work as Right Leg from * to **.

Arms

Cast on 6sts, work i-cord until arm measures 11.5cm (4½in). Sl1, k1, psso, k2, k2tog. (4sts) Cut yarn, thread end through sts. Sew the arms to the side of the body working a couple of sts with sewing thread to secure.

Hair

Using yarn C, cast on 36sts. Work in garter stitch for 2 rows. *Cast on 3, cast off 3, cast off 2sts. Slip st that's on RH needle onto LH**, rep from * to ** to last set, cast on 3, cast off 3, cast off last 2sts. Stitch the hair evenly onto the head with sewing thread, tie extra lengths at the back into a pony tail.

Simple dress

Using yarn Dress, cast on 34sts and divide over 3 needles; n1 – 12sts, n2 – 10sts, n3 – 12sts. Join in the round, being careful not to twist. Work evenly, knitting every rnd, for 12 rnds.

Rnd 13: (dec) (K3, sl1, k1, psso, k2tog) twice, k6, (sl1, k1, psso, k2tog, k3) twice. (26sts) Work evenly, knitting every rnd, for 12 rnds.

Rnd 26: (dec) K6, sl1, k1, psso, k2tog, k6, sl1, k1, psso, k2tog, k6. (22sts) Work evenly, knitting every rnd, for 3 rnds.
Shape the sleeves as follows:

Rnd 30: (dec) K4, cast off 4sts, k5, cast off 4sts, k3. (14sts)

Rnd 31: (inc) K4, backward loop (BL) cast on 4sts, k6, BL cast on 4sts, k4. (22sts)

Rnd 32: K22.
Cast off.

2. Dress the doll. Embroider eyes using doubled strands of white sewing thread. Make a single stitch for the eye and as the thread emerges out onto the right side of the face, snip ends as eyelashes. Cut a tiny felt triangle for the mouth and stitch onto the face with a couple of tiny stitches.

BUSY BEE CUSHION
by Louise Butt

You Will Need:

3.75mm (US size 5)
knitting needles

◆

Four 4mm (US size 6)
double-pointed needles

◆

3 x 100g balls yellow yarn
1 x 50g ball black yarn
Patons Fab DK Canary (02305)
Patons Diploma Gold DK Black (06183)

1. Knit the cushion
following the pattern below:

Front
Cast on 110sts in yellow yarn
using 3.75mm needles.
Starting with a k row work
16 rows in st st.
Place intarsia chart: K16 then start
chart. (Note: start counting the sts
from the bottom right corner, these
sts are in addition to the first 16 you
worked at the start of the row.) Once
chart is finished, cont in st st until the
length of your knitting measures the
same as the width. Then cast off.

Back
Cast on 110sts in yellow yarn
and work in st st until knitting
measures the same length
as the front. Cast off.

2. For the cushion edging
make a length of i-cord
following the pattern below:

Using two 4mm dpns and black yarn
cast on 4sts. K all sts, but don't turn
the needle. Instead slide all the sts
to the other end of the dpn and with
right side facing, pull the working
yarn to give it a slight tension and k
the 4sts, then slide worked sts to
the end of the needle again. Cont.

3. Produce a tube of knitting
that is long enough to fit around
all four sides of the cushion.

4. Darn in all ends and join
three sides of the cushion. Insert
a cushion pad to fit, then sew the
remaining side closed. Attach
the i-cord to the edge using
backstitch to conceal the seam.

CUTE HANGING HEART
by Dorothy Wood

You Will Need:

4mm (US size 6)
knitting needles

◆

1 x 50g ball lime yarn
Patons Dreamtime DK Lime (04952)

◆

Fuchsia, gold and white felt

1. Knit two hearts following the pattern below:

Using 4mm knitting needles and lime yarn cast on 2sts.
Row 1: (WS) Knit, purl to end.
Row 2: (RS) Increase by knitting into the front and back (kf&b) of both of the stitches on the needle. (4sts)
Row 3: Purl to end.
Row 4: Kf&b of 1st st, knit to last st, kf&b. (6sts)
Row 5: Purl to end.
Repeat rows 4 and 5 until 18sts.
Knit 6 rows stocking stitch.
*Knit 9 and turn, purl to end of row. K2tog tbl, knit to last 2sts k2tog. Purl.
Repeat last 2 rows to 3sts rem, cast off knit wise on the purl side. Rejoin yarn and work other the half of the heart from * to match.

2. Block the knitted hearts by lightly steam pressing on the reverse side. Using lime yarn and a blunt needle, sew together around the edges leaving a gap on a straight side. Stuff with chopped up scrap yarn or stuffing. Sew the gap closed.

3. Draw 2cm (¾in), 3cm (1⅛in) and 4cm (1½in) diameter circles onto three different colours of felt.

4. Cut out the felt circles; use pinking shears to cut out the middle circle just outside the marked line. Layer the felt onto the stuffed heart shape. Unravel some yarn and use two strands to sew through the felt and heart out the other side. Sew back through the felt. Tie at the front and trim the ends. Sew a length of yarn at the 'V' of the heart at the top. Tie the yarn ends together and trim.

KNITTING

CELEBRATION BUNTING

by Rowena Lane

You Will Need:

4mm (US size 6)
knitting needles

◆

1 x 50g ball blue yarn
1 x 50g ball red yarn
1 x 50g ball white yarn
Patons Diploma Gold DK
Royal (06170), Red (06151)
and White (06187)

◆

Satin ribbon
(1.5cm/⅝in wide)

1. Make as many bunting flags as you require following the pattern below and making an equal number from each colour yarn.

Make a slip knot and place on LH needle.
Row 1: (RS) Increase by knitting into the front and back (kf&b) of slip knot. (2sts)
Row 2: Sl1, kf&b. (3sts)
Row 3: Sl1, kf&b, k1. (4sts)
Row 4: Sl1, kf&b, k2. (5sts)
Row 5: Sl1, kf&b, knit to end. (6sts)
Repeat row 5 until 12sts on needle.
Knit 2 rows.
Rows 14–15: As row 5.

Rows 16–17: Sl1, knit to end.
Repeat last 4 rows until 33sts on needle.
Knit 3 rows.
Make buttonholes:
Row 37: K3 (cast off 3, k4) to end.
Row 38: K2 (inc in next st, yarn over, inc in next st, k3) repeat to end.
Knit 3 rows.
Cast off.

2. Lay out the bunting flags in a row. Stitch the top 1cm (⅜in) of the outside edges of the flags together to form a continuous length. Thread ribbon through the buttonholes, leaving approximately 30cm (12in) at each end for hanging.

KNITTING

KITTEN MITTENS
by Claire Garland

You Will Need:

Four 5mm (US size 8)
double-pointed needles

◆

1 x 100g ball pink yarn
Rowan Cocoon Petal (823)

◆

Cream, emerald green, lilac,
grey and black stranded
cotton (floss)
DMC colours 726, 562,
341, 415 and 310

◆

Mini blue bows
Modern Retro

1. Knit the mittens following the knitting pattern below:

Cast on 28sts and divide over 3 needles; n1 – 9sts, n2 – 10sts, n3 – 9sts.
Join in the round, being careful not to twist.
Work evenly, knitting every rnd, for 18 rnds.
For right-hand mitten: K10sts, place stitch marker – this marker tallies with the marker on the motif chart – k18.
For left-hand mitten: K24sts, place stitch marker – this marker tallies with the marker on the motif chart – k4

Divide for thumb.
Rnd 20: K18, knit into front and back of next st (kf&b), K1, kf&b, k26. (30sts)
Rnd 21: K30.
Rnd 22: Place row marker, kf&b, k4, kf&b, place row marker, k26. (32sts)
Rnd 23: K32.
Rnd 24: kf&b, k6, kf&b, k26. (34sts)
Rnd 25: K34.
Rnds 26–32: Cont to increase on every alternate round at beg of thumb (after first row marker) and end of thumb (before second row marker), until the thumb has 16 sts. (42sts)
Rnd 33: K16, slide last 16 (these are the thumb sts) onto a spare length of yarn. K26.

Divide remaining stitches evenly onto 3 needles and work 1 round, leaving thumb stitches on spare yarn.
Work 4 rnds k1, p1 rib.
Cast off in rib. Weave in the end.
Rejoin 16 thumb sts to needles, dividing over 3 needles. Pick up one st at beg of thumb sts, k16, pick up 2 sts along hand junction, join in rnd as before. (19sts)
Work 3 rnds st st. Cast off.
Following the chart, work the motif using Swiss darning beginning from the marker position (red cross) and using the stranded cotton threaded in a blunt needle.
Stick then sew on a mini blue bow at the neck of the kitten motif.

IPAD COSY

by Rowena Lane

You Will Need:

5mm (US size 8)
knitting needles

◆

1 x 100g ball blue yarn **(MC)**
1 x 100g ball
variegated yarn **(C)**
Rowan Cocoon Misty Blue (827) and
Patons Fab DK Rainbow (02085)

◆

Button

1. Knit the iPad cover
following the pattern below:

Back
Cast on 32sts in MC.
Row 1: K4, p4 to end.
Row 2: P4, k4 to end.
Repeat Rows 1 and 2
three times (6 rows worked).
Row 7: P4, k4 to end.
Row 8: K4, p4 to end.
Repeat rows 7 and 8 three more times.
These 12 rows form the pattern.
Rep until work measures 27cm (10⅝in).
Shape flap:
Row 1: K1, K2tog, k to
last 3sts, K2tbl, K1.

Row 2: K to end of row.
Repeat rows 1and 2 three times. (26sts)
Change to yarn C and continue
decreasing on alternate rows
as above for next 4 rows.
Change back to MC (use doubled)
and cont in patt until 10sts
rem on needle. K next row.
Make buttonhole:
Row 1: K3, cast off 4sts, knit to end.
Row 2: K3, Yfwd, K3. (7sts)
Row 3: Knit to end.
Row 4: K1, K2tog, K1,
K2tog tbl, K1. (5sts)
Row 5: Knit to end.
Row 6: K1, K3tog, K1. (3sts)
Cast off.

Front
Using yarn C, cast on 32sts.
Work as for back until
24cm (9½in) long.
Next rows k to end, until work
measures 27cm (10⅝in).
Cast off.

2. Stitch the front onto the
back to make the pouch.
Fold the flap over the front,
mark the button position,
then sew the button on.

CAMERA BOOK COVER

by Louise Butt

You Will Need:

3.75mm (US size 5)
knitting needles

◆

2 x 50g balls black yarn
1 x 50g ball white yarn
Patons Diploma Gold DK Black
(06183) and White (06187)

1. Knit the photograph album book cover following the pattern below:

Using 3.75mm needles and black yarn, cast on 90sts and work 4 rows garter stitch.
Row 1: K.
Row 2: K6, p to last 6sts, k6. (Work these 2 rows throughout while including the chart, to give you a flat selvedge.) Work a further 6 rows in black.

Place intarsia chart: Work 20sts, then place chart. (Note: start counting the sts from the bottom right corner, these sts are in addition to the first 20 you worked at the start of the row.) Once chart is complete, continue with Rows 1 and 2 until knitting from last row of garter stitch measures 21cm (8¼in). Work 4 rows garter stitch. Cast off.

2. With wrong side facing, pin out the knitted panel using glass headed pins to the correct size. Cover with a damp cloth and press gently using a steam iron. With the wrong side of your work facing you, fold over each edge by 4cm (1½in) and join using backstitch above the bottom section of garter stitch and below the top section of garter stitch. Insert your photograph album.

SNAKE SCARF
by Zoe Larkins

You Will Need:

8mm (US size 11)
knitting needles

◆

2 x 100g balls variegated yarn
Rowan Colourscape Chunky Ghost (435)

◆

Red, white and black felt

◆

Violet ribbon

◆

Toy filling

1. Cast on 20sts using 8mm needles working in stocking stitch (one row knit, one row purl) until required length is achieved.

2. When you have reached the desired length for your scarf, start decreasing your stitches following the pattern below:

Row 1: K3, K2tog tbl, K2tog, K6, K2tog, K2tog tbl, K to end. (16sts)
Row 2: Purl to end.
Row 3: K2, K2tog tbl, K2tog, K4, K2tog, K2tog tbl, K to end. (12sts)
Row 4: As row 2.
Row 5: K1, K2tog tbl, K2tog, K6, K2tog, K2tog tbl, K to end. (8sts)

Row 6: As row 2.
Row 7: K1, Sl1, K2tog, psso, Sl2 knitwise, K1, psso, K1. (4sts)
Row 8: As row 2
Row 9: K1, P2tog, K1. (3sts)
Row 10: K3tog. (1sts)
Break off yarn and pull through. Sew up the sides of the scarf from the tail end, as though you are making a tube.

3. Approximately 20cm (8in) from the end, stop and stitch around the tube to gather in and make your snake's 'neck'.

4. Stitch from the head to the neck, leaving you with a pocket that you will fill with the toy filling.

5. Once the snake's head is firmly filled, stitch the gap closed. Attach some felt circle eyes cut from white and black felt. Cut a tongue from red felt and stitch in place. Tie a smart ribbon bow around the snake's neck to finish.

STRIPEY BLING CUSHION
by Jo Irving

You Will Need:

3.25mm (US size 3)
knitting needles

◆

1 x 100g ball green yarn **(MC)**
1 x 25g ball purple yarn **(C)**
Patons 100% Cotton 4 Ply Apple
(01205) and Rowan Kidsilk
Haze Blackcurrant (641)

◆

Fabric for cushion back:
One piece 50cm x 50cm
(20in x 20in)
Liberty Art Mayfair Mosaic Flower Blue

◆

Green sewing thread
Gutermann colour 582

1. Divide the kid silk haze (yarn C) into two separate balls to make it easier for you to knit with two threads of this fine yarn.

2. Knit the cushion front following the pattern below:

Using yarn MC cast on 105sts (thumb method) and starting with a knit row knit st st (knit on right side RS, purl on wrong side WS) for 10 rows.

Row 11: Using two strands of yarn C, knit one row.
Row 12: Yarn MC for 8 rows.
Row 20: Yarn C for 2 rows.
Row 22: Yarn MC for 8 rows.
Row 30: Yarn C for 3 rows.
Row 33: Yarn MC for 8 rows.
Row 41: Yarn C for 4 rows.
Repeat this pattern until your knitted piece measures the size of your cushion pad (approximately 46cm x 46cm/18in x 18in). Cast off and sew in the loose yarn ends.

3. Press your fabric square and carefully press your knitted square. With right sides facing, sew the knitted square to the fabric leaving one edge open.

4. Slip the cushion cover over the cushion pad. Over sew the open seam to join the knitted and fabric edge, leaving a neat seam.

KNITTED CHARMS
by Claire Garland

You Will Need:

Four 3mm (US size 2)
double-pointed needles

◆

1 x 100g ball yellow yarn **(A)**
1 x 50g ball pink yarn **(B)**
1 x 50g ball red yarn **(C)**
1 x 50g ball purple yarn **(D)**
1 x 50g ball white yarn **(E)**
Rowan Creative Focus Worsted
Saffron (03810), Rowan Pure Yarn
DK Hyacinth (026), Rowan Baby
Alpaca DK Cherry (224), Rowan
Baby Alpaca DK Blossom (225) and
Rowan Purelife British Sheep Breeds
DK Bluefaced Leicester (780)

◆

Blue felt

◆

White sewing thread
Gutermann colour 800

◆

Row marker

◆

Toy filling

◆

Buttons (optional)

1. Knit the bird, flower and heart charms following the patterns below. (Note: the charms use only very small amounts of yarn so you will have plenty to make several of each if you choose to.

Bird charm:
In yarn E cast on 8sts.
*Step 1: Hold needle with sts in left hand (LH).
Step 2: Hold 2 empty dpns parallel in right hand.
Step 3: Slip 1st stitch onto the dpn closest to you and off the LH needle. Slip next stitch onto the dpn furthest away and off the LH needle. ****** Repeat Steps 1–3 until all 8sts are divided onto the 2 parallel dpns. Slide sts to other end of dpns. Work in the round over 2 dpns using a 3rd dpn to knit with.
Rnd 1: Beg with the 4sts at the back, k8.
Rnd 2: (inc) Kf&b, k2, kf&b, kf&b, k2, kf&b. (12sts – 6sts on each dpn)
Rnds 3, 5, 7, 9: K.
Rnds 4, 6, 8: Increase 4sts on each rnd; increasing 1st at beg and end on each dpn. (24sts)
Rnd 10: (inc) Kf&b, k11, k11, kf&b. (26sts)
Rnd 11: (inc) Kf&b, k11, kf&b, kf&b, k11, kf&b. (30sts)
Rnd 12: (inc) Kf&b, k14, k14, kf&b. (32sts)
Rnd 13: (inc) Kf&b, k15, k15, kf&b. (34sts)
Rnd 14: (inc) Kf&b, k14,

k2tog, k2tog, k14, kf&b.
Rep last round once.
Cut yarn leaving a 23cm (9in) length.

Making up
Very lightly stuff the little bird with toy filling or scrap yarn.
Graft to join.
Cut an equilateral triangle (approximately 1.3cm/½in each side) from blue felt for the beak, fold in half, point to point, and sew on with the two halves touching the bird (the fold becomes the top of the beak).
Cut a 2.5cm (1in) diameter circle then cut the circle in half for the wings and oversew the straight edge onto the sides of the bird's body.
Sew a stitch or two using a length of contrasting yarn for the eyes.

Flower charm:
Double petal
In yarn A cast on 6sts.
Divide over 2 dpns as Bird Charm from * to **.
Repeat Steps 1–3 until all 6sts are divided onto the 2 parallel dpns.
Slide sts to other end of dpns.
Work in the round over two dpns using a 3rd dpn to knit with.
Rnd 1: (inc) Beg with the 3sts at the back, *kf&b, k1, kf&b, kf&b, k1, kf&b. (10sts)
Rnd 2: K10.
Rnd 3: (inc) Kf&b, k3, kf&b, kf&b, k3, kf&b. (14sts)
Rnd 4: K14. Place marker.
Rep last rnd 7 times.

Rnd 12: (dec) Sl1, k1, psso, k3, k2tog, sl1, k1, psso, k3, k2tog. (10sts)
Stuff petal with toy filling or scrap yarn.
Rnd 13: (dec) Sl1, k1, psso, k1, k2tog, sl1, k1, psso, k1, k2tog. (6sts) **
Rnd 14: K6.
Rep last rnd three times.
Rep from * to ** (Rnds 1 – 13) once.
Cut yarn leaving a 10cm (3⅞in) length.
Graft to join.

Flower centre
In yarn B cast on 6sts.
Divide over 2 dpns as Bird Charm from * to **.
Continue to make as Flower Charm Petals up to Rnd 13 (at **)
Cut yarn leaving a 10cm (3⅞in) length.
Graft to join.
Make 2 more double petals.
Stack all 3 double petals on top of each other and push a threaded yarn needle through the centres to join, work a few stitches to secure the stack then sew the flower centre to the middle of the stack. Splay the petals outwards to form the flower.

Heart charm:
In yarn C cast on 4 sts. Divide over 2 dpns as Bird Charm from * to **.
Row 3: Repeat Steps 1–3 until all 4sts are divided onto the 2 parallel dpns. Slide sts to other end of dpns.
Work in the round over 2 dpns

using a 3rd dpn to knit with.
Rnd 1: (inc) Beg with the 2sts at the back, kf&b 4 times. (8sts)
Rnd 2: K8.
Rnd 3: (inc) Kf&b, k2, kf&b, kf&b, k2, kf&b. (12sts)
Rnds 4, 6, 8, 10, 12: K.
Rnds 5, 7, 9, 11: Increase 4sts on each rnd; increasing 1st at beg and end on each dpn. (28sts)
Rnds 13, 14: K.
Rnd 15: K7, slip next 14sts off needles and onto a length of spare yarn, knit next 7.
Rnd 16: (dec) *Sl1, k1, psso, k3, k2tog, sl1, k1, psso, k3, k2tog. (10sts)
Rnd 17: K10.
Rnd 18: (dec) Sl1, k1, psso, k1, k2tog, sl1, k1, psso, k1, k2tog. (6sts)
Cut yarn leaving a 10cm (3⅞in) length.
Graft to join. **

Making up
Very lightly stuff the heart with toy filling or scrap yarn.
Divide 14sts from other side of heart equally over 2 needles, rejoin yarn, K14 then knit from * to ** (Rnds 16 to end of pattern), completing the stuffing just before joining.
If there is a tiny gap between the two bumps work a little stitch to close.

2. Join the charms together with spare lengths of yarn or thin ribbon, separating the charms with buttons if you wish.

PRETTY PEG BAG
by Louise Butt

You Will Need:

3.75mm (US size 5)
knitting needles

◆

3 x 50g balls dark blue yarn
1 x 50g ball aqua yarn
Patons Diploma Gold DK Navy
(06167) and Aqua (06243)

◆

Row marker

◆

Coat hanger

1. Knit the peg bag
following the pattern below:

Using 3.75mm knitting needles
cast on 70sts in dark blue yarn
and work 6 rows garter stitch.

Start moss stitch
Row 1: (K1, p1) to end of row.
Row 2: (P1, k1) to end of row.
Rep these two rows until
knitting measures 9cm
(3½in) ending with Row 2.
Next row: Work moss stitch
for 34sts, yarn over needle,
k2tog, moss st to end of row.
Continue in moss st until knitting
measures 40cm (15½in).
Place row marker and work 12
rows more of moss stitch.
Place intarsia chart: Note: all sts
of chart (even those represented

by white squares) are worked in
st st, with a moss st border either
side. There is a 5 row border of st
st above and below the peg image.
Work 13sts in moss stitch, P
across the first 44sts of the
chart, moss stitch to end. This
represents row 1 of the chart.
Once you have finished the chart
including the 5-row st st border
above the last row of the peg image,
work 12 rows of moss stitch
Then work 6 rows of garter stitch.
Cast off.

2. Embroider the peg spring
using backstitch, then gently press
the chart area on the reverse of
the knitting. Darn in all ends.

3. With right sides facing join
the cast on and cast off edges
by 7.5cm (3in) on each side.
Fold the bag so that the hanger
opening is situated on the top fold.
Smooth the peg bag flat and then
sew along both selvedges. Turn right
side out and insert coat hanger.

KNITTING

KINDLE CASE
by Lisa Fordham

You Will Need:

3.5mm (US size 4)
knitting needles

◆

2 x 50g balls dark
purple yarn **(MC)**
1 x 50g ball pink yarn **(C)**
Patons Diploma Gold DK Charcoal
(06298) and Cyclamen (06123)

◆

Pink felt

◆

Two square buttons

1. Knit the kindle case following the pattern below:

Front
Cast on 23sts in MC yarn.
Start moss stitch:
Row 1: (K1, p1) to end of row.
Row 2: As row 1.
Work 12 rows in pattern.
Change to C yarn and work 8 rows.
Change back to main colour
and work until knitting measures 14cm (5½in). Cast off.

Back
Cast on 23sts in MC yarn and work in moss stitch until back measures 24cm (9½in) to allow for flap. Cast off.

2. Make a lining from pink felt to match the size of the knitted cover.

3. Place lining inside the knitted cover and finish by using blanket stitch to attach the lining to the inside of the flap.

4. Attach the buttons to the front and make two small holes in the flap for the buttonholes. Blanket stitch around the buttonholes to give a clean edge.

KNITTING

PAPERCRAFT

VINTAGE TEACUP CARD

by Prudence Rogers

You Will Need:

Stiff white card

◆

Patterned paper
Tilda Summer Blues

◆

Decorative edge punch
Martha Stewart doily lace

◆

White paper

◆

Glue stick

◆

Gold pen

1. Using the template, cut out the teacup design from thick white card with a craft knife. Fold the card in half down the centre.

2. Cut out a piece of floral patterned paper following the bowl section of the teacup template and glue onto the white folded card.

3. Cut out a piece of striped paper following the lower portion of the template and glue in place.

4. Use the edge punch to cut a scalloped strip 2cm (¾in) deep along the edge of the white paper. Ensure that your strip is long enough to cover the width of the cup.

5. Glue the white paper to the top of the card and trim the edges to fit. Draw decorative details on the top rim, base and handle with a gold pen.

6. If desired, repeat steps 2–5 to decorate the back of the card in the same way.

PAPERCRAFT

SPRINGTIME CARDS
by Debbie Pyne

You Will Need:

A4 (US letter) white
cards and envelopes

◆

Patterned paper
K & Company

◆

Flower card toppers
K & Company

◆

Glue stick

1. Fold the pre-folded card from the card pack, choosing either white or cream.

2. Select pieces of patterned paper and carefully cut shapes to fit neatly against the edge of the card; stick down. Next select your circular toppers and stick onto the card and over the top of the patterned paper.

3. Select your butterfly toppers and stick these onto the card and patterned paper.

4. Using a fine line black pen, or alternatively a gold or silver pen, draw onto the card to help to bring the pattern to life. (You can draw very lightly onto the card first in pencil if you like.)

PAPERCRAFT

BUTTERFLY PRESENT TOPPER
by Jennifer Forster

You Will Need:

Pastel paper

◆

Pastel vellum

◆

Sticky foam pads

◆

Champagne ultra fine glitter (optional)

1. Print out or trace the two butterfly templates. Draw around the butterfly templates onto the pastel paper and the pastel vellum and cut out.

2. Adhere a foam pad under the smaller butterfly's body.

3. Stick the smaller butterfly on top of the larger butterfly, making sure that the wings are left unstuck.

4. Adhere the double butterfly to the present with sticky foam pads for dimensional effect. Add glitter for extra sparkle!

PAPERCRAFT

PRETTY PAPER BUNTING
by Prudence Rogers

You Will Need:

Patterned paper
Tilda Fruit Garden

◆

Decorative ribbons
Tilda Fruit Garden

◆

Decorative edge punch
Martha Stewart double scallop

◆

Glue stick

◆

Hole punch

1. Using the template, cut two triangles for each bunting flag from co-ordinating patterned papers. The more triangles you choose to make, the longer your bunting will be.

2. Cut strips of striped dark pink paper 2.5cm (1in) wide. You will need four strips for each of your triangles. Punch the strips with a scallop border punch to create a decorative edge. Glue two strips wrong sides together to make them double-sided.

3. Glue one strip to each side of a triangle on the wrong side of the paper. The scalloped edge should overhang the edge of the triangle by about 1cm (⅜in). Glue the matching triangle of patterned paper over the glued edges of the strips to cover them up and create a double-sided bunting flag. Repeat for the remaining paper triangles and strips.

4. Use a hole punch to cut out one hole on either side of the top edge of your bunting flags.

5. Cut lengths of ribbon 60cm (23⅝in) long. Thread a length of ribbon through the right-hand hole of one bunting flag, from the back to the front. Put the other end through the left-hand hole of the next bunting flag and tie the two ends together in a bow.

6. Trim the ends of the ribbon so that they are even, creating an inverted V-shape. Continue in this way to add more flags until your bunting is the desired length.

PAPERCRAFT

CUPCAKE GIFT CARDS
by Jeni Hennah

You Will Need:

Pearlescent card

◆

Patterned card and
cupcake card toppers

◆

Glue stick

1. Cut a rectangle measuring 7.5cm x 15cm (3in x 6in) from your chosen background card and fold in half.

2. Choose your papers for the cupcake and for the cupcakecase. Cut out one case piece and four cake pieces from your selected papers using the templates. Fold each of the four cake pieces in half horizontally.

3. Take one folded cake piece and glue another folded piece to it, aligning the back of each half. Continue to attach the remaining cake pieces in the same way until you have a concertina semicircle shape, but do not glue the last two pieces together.

4. Flatten the concertina so that you have one semicircle shape with a front and back.

5. Glue the case piece to the background card. Stick the back of the flattened concertina cake piece to the card, overlapping the case slightly.

6. Choose a topper and glue on top of the cake design. Gently pull the layers of the concertina cake piece out to create a dimensional shape. This can be flattened again for posting.

PAPERCRAFT

SHABBY CHIC GIFT BAG
by Jane Millard

You Will Need:

Patterned paper
Tilda Fruit Garden

◆

Checked satin ribbon
Tilda Pink/White

◆

Decorative edge punch
Martha Stewart doily lace

◆

Scalloped circle punch
Martha Stewart Punch
All Over The Page

◆

Brads

◆

**Double-sided tape
and glue stick**

1. From green patterned paper, cut a strip measuring 30cm x 8cm (11⅞in x 3½in) and two squares measuring 10cm x 10cm (3⅞in x 3⅞in). Score the strip 2cm (¾in) in from each edge and fold. Score every 10cm (3⅞in) and fold. Cut notches and fold up to attach to the squares by gluing tabs to the box sides.

2. To make the handle cut a strip of green paper measuring 5.5cm x 30cm (2⅛in x 11⅞in).

3. Punch the edges of the handle strip using the decorative edge punch and add a strip of pink patterned paper along the centre measuring 2.5cm x 30cm (1in x 11⅞in). Attach to the inside of the bag.

4. Punch along the edge of a strip of dark pink striped paper measuring 6cm x 30cm (2⅜in x 11⅞in) and fix around the top of the bag.

5. Tape a strip of ribbon around the bag and tie ribbon around the handle. Punch five scalloped circles from pale pink patterned paper and fix them together by piercing through the centre of each one and securing with a brad. Spray with water and scrunch each layer starting with the top one to create a flower. Let dry.

6. Cut two small green leaves from paper. Glue to the bag and glue the flower on top.

PRETTY GIFT-JAR WRAP

by Jennifer Grace

You Will Need:

Pearlescent card

♦

Bunting clear stamp set
Let's Go

♦

Decorative edge punch
Martha Stewart doily lace

♦

Black ink pad
Tsukineko Memento Tuxedo Black

♦

Ultra-adhesive tape
and glue stick

♦

Clean jar with lid

1. Measure the circumference of a jar that has been cleaned and dried. Cut a piece of blue card measuring 6cm (2⅜in) tall, and the width as long as your jar circumference. Cut a piece of green card 2.5cm (1in) tall, by the same width as the jar circumference, minus 3cm (1⅛in).

2. Stamp flag poles using black ink, about a third of the way along from the left and right edges of the blue card.

3. Punch a decorative border along the green card's long top edge and attach to the bottom of the blue card with ultra-adhesive tape.

4. Stamp small triangles onto coloured card and stick onto the blue card in a bunting pattern; start in the top centre and form an upside down arc to finish in the right-hand third of the card. Attach the decorated blue card panel to your jar using ultra-adhesive tape to ensure it stays in place.

5. Cut a 6cm x 3cm (2⅜in x 1⅛in) piece of blue card; adhere with ultra-adhesive tape over the join at the back. Then cut and punch a 2.5cm x 3cm (1in x 1⅛in) piece of green card to attach on top, so your 'grass' meets up. Fill your jar with sweets or goodies and gift it!

PAPERCRAFT

SUMMER PAPER CHAIN
by Verity Graves-Morris

You Will Need:

Patterned paper
Tilda Summer Blues

◆

Double-sided tape

1. Cut your paper into strips measuring 30cm x 2.5cm (12in x 1in) wide. The more strips you cut, the longer your chain will be.

2. Cut off pieces of double-sided tape approximately 1.3cm (½in) in length and stick down at the tip of each strip.

3. Taking one paper strip, peel off the paper on the double-sided tape, then loop over the strip and secure it to the tape so that it forms a chain link.

4. Thread the next paper strip through the first chain link, peel off the double-sided tape and loop round the paper strip to form a second chain link.

5. Repeat the process until the chain is the length that you require. There are approximately nine chains per metre/yard – invite your friends in to help.

PAPERCRAFT

FUN ANIMAL CARDS
by Jeni Hennah

You Will Need:

Pearlescent card

◆

Glue stick

◆

Sticky foam pads

1. Cut out the template pieces needed for your animal.
For Archie: Cut out one body in pink, two wings in dark blue, one beak in black, two eyes in white and one moon in gold.
For Phoebe: Cut out one body in orange, two fins in purple, one tail in purple, one mouth in red and one eye in white.

2. Cut out any additional shapes needed for your animal.
For Archie: Cut four 6mm (¼in) wide strips in pink, two pupils in black using a standard hole punch and one tree branch approximately 2cm (¾in) wide in brown.
For Phoebe: Cut four 6mm (¼in) wide strips in red, one pupil in black and three bubbles in white using a standard hole punch, and some seaweed in green.

3. Stick all the shapes required for each animal together.
For Archie: Glue two pink strips to each wing and trim the edges with scissors. Glue the two wings to each side of the body. Stick on the eyes and then beak, then add the pupils to the eyes, slightly off centre to create character.
For Phoebe: Glue four red strips to the body and trim the edges with scissors. Attach the mouth and tail behind the body (you can use tape to hold this in place if necessary). Glue the two fins to the top and middle of the body. Stick on the eyes and add the pupil.

4. Cut a rectangle of pearlescent card measuring 10cm x 20cm (3⅞in x 7⅞in) and fold in half – use black for Archie the owl and blue for Phoebe the fish.

5. Stick the background shapes onto the card – the tree branch for Archie and seaweed for Phoebe. Attach your animal to the card using sticky foam pads. Stick down the other decorative shapes – moon for Archie and bubbles for Phoebe.

PAPERCRAFT

PAPER GARLAND

by Kirsty Neale

You Will Need:

Patterned paper
Cath Kidston stationery box

◆

Decorative tape
Cath Kidston

◆

Decorative edge punch
Martha Stewart doily lace

◆

Stranded cotton (floss) to
match the patterned papers

◆

1 x 50g ball green yarn
Rowan Yarn Cotton Elf (946)

1. Cut out pieces of paper, roughly 8cm x 12cm (3½in x 4¾in) – they can be bigger or smaller than this if you'd prefer. Use a mixture of plain and patterned papers. Punch a lacy border along one short edge of some of the pieces.

2. Snip extra pieces of paper into narrow strips and punch a lace border along one or both edges. Glue these onto some of the flags to decorate.

3. Decorate the remaining flags with simple stitching, paper scraps and strips of tape.

4. Fold over 1.5cm (⅝in) at the top edge of each paper flag. Stitch along the bottom of the folded section, to make a narrow channel.

5. Cut a piece or the green yarn and thread it through the channel at the top of each flag. Arrange the flags evenly along the length of the string to display.

PAPERCRAFT

UNION JACK CARD
by Jane Millard

You Will Need:

Patterned paper
Tilda Summer Blues

◆

White scalloped
cards and envelopes
13cm x 18cm (5in x 7in)

◆

Pink checked ribbon

◆

Blue and pink
pearlescent paper

◆

Glue stick

1. Cut a piece of blue rose patterned paper to measure 11cm x 16cm (4⅜in x 6⅜in).

2. Cut two strips of white patterned paper about 1.5cm (⅝in) wide and fix in a diagonal across the card. Add strips of pink card cut to 5mm (³⁄₁₆in) on top. Trim at the corners.

3. Add two strips of white paper cut to 3cm (1⅛in) wide in a cross through the centre of the panel. Add ribbon on top and tuck behind. Stick the panel to a rectangle of pink card cut to 11.5cm x 16.5cm (4½in x 6½in) .

4. Glue the panel to the front of the scalloped card; add ribbon bow.

PAPERCRAFT

FLORAL GREETINGS CARD
by Debbie Pyne

You Will Need:

C6 white cards
and envelopes

◆

Springtime paper
and vellum pack

◆

Sticky foam pads

◆

Squizzers precision scissors

◆

Glue stick

1. Using the paper selection pack, select a piece for the grass. Tear gently so it covers approximately a third of the card, leaving a 6mm (¼in) gap around the edges. Stick down using glue stick. Cut or tear a smaller piece of vellum, covering about a sixth of the page with a 6mm (¼in) gap around the edge and stick on top of the first layer.

2. Choose papers for the tall flowers. Cut out four circle shapes and four smaller circles from contrasting paper for the centres. Glue larger circles straight onto the card; use sticky foam pads for the circle centres.

3. Choose paper for the poppies and cut out 18 circles (six 1.5cm/⅝in and the rest slightly smaller). Stick the larger circles straight onto the card, then stick on the additional smaller circles using a foam pad between each layer to create dimension.

4. Cut out petals for the remaining two flowers (you will need 10 per flower).

5. Stick the first layer of petals straight onto the card and use foam pads to stick down the additional petals on top. Cut out smaller circle centres in contrasting paper and stick on using foam pads.

6. Using a black pen, draw on the flower stems and add centres to the poppies. You do not have to worry about making the flower stems perfect!

PAPERCRAFT

PAPER GIFT BAG
by Jennifer Forster

You Will Need:

Patterned card or paper

◆

Ribbon

◆

Pink mesh butterflies
Colour Connection

◆

Glue stick

1. Following the diagram, cut out two pieces of card 2.5cm x 11cm (1in x 4⅜in) and stick in panel A and B to strengthen. Fold down flap C and stick.

2. Fold side D over to meet side E. Glue right side of tab D and stick to the inside of side E so that the side D joins to make the body of the bag.

3. Looking at the bottom of the bag, push in panels F and then fold down the other flaps one on top of the other and glue. To strengthen, place a piece of card in the bottom of the bag.

4. Punch holes for the ribbon handles 1.5cm (⅝in) from the top of the bag and 3cm (1⅛in) in from each side, and roughly 5cm (2in) apart. Cut two pieces of ribbon to about 15cm (6in) each, thread through and knot inside to fasten.

PAPERCRAFT

PATCHWORK
&
QUILTING

QUILTED COASTERS
by Linda Clements

You Will Need:

Fabric for coaster top:
Nine pieces 5.7cm x 5.7cm
(2¼in x 2¼in)
Tilda Christmas House Folklore Red,
Tanya Whelan Delilah Paisley Green,
Tanya Whelan Delilah Dots Pink and
Tilda Cotton Fabric White

Fabric for coaster back:
One piece 15.2cm x 15.2cm
(6in x 6in)
Tanya Whelan Delilah Dots Pink

◆

Wadding (batting)

◆

Dark pink and green
stranded cotton (floss)
DMC colours 309 and 319

1. Take the four polka dot squares, the four print squares and the white square and arrange as shown in the photograph. Using 6mm (¼in) seams, sew the nine squares together. Press the seams.

2. Copy the quilting pattern and tape it to a window. Tape the patchwork on top, right side up, so the pattern shows through in the middle of the patchwork. Use a pencil to *lightly* trace the quilting pattern onto the fabric.

3. Take the 15.2cm (6in) square of wadding and safety pin on the back of the patchwork. Quilt using three strands of stranded cotton. Start with a dark pink French knot in the flower centre, then quilt the traced pattern, stitching through both layers, working the flowers in dark pink and leaves in green.

4. Place the patchwork right side *up*. Put the square of backing fabric right side *down* on top of the patchwork and pin together.

5. Trim the wadding and backing to the same size as the patchwork. Machine stitch together all the way around the edge leaving a gap of about 5.cm (2in) in one side. Trim the corners a little, turn through to the right side and press.

6. Turn the edges of the gap inwards neatly and hand sew together with little stitches and matching thread. Machine sew all around the edge of the mat for a neat, firm edge.

PATCHWORK AND QUILTING

MINI-SQUARES CUSHION
by Marion Elliot

You Will Need:

Fat quarter fabric pack
Heather Bailey Nicey Jane

◆

White sewing thread
Gutermann colour 800

1. For the patchwork on the cushion front, make yourself a card template measuring 5cm (2in) square.

2. Cut 64 squares of fabric. Pin the squares together along one edge, with right sides facing, to make a strip of eight patches. Machine stitch together, using a 1cm (⅜in) seam allowance. Repeat to make seven more strips of eight patches. Press open the seams.

3. Pin two strips together along one long edge, right sides facing and matching seam lines exactly. Machine stitch together. Repeat to join the rest of the strips together, to form a square of eight rows of eight patches. This is the cushion front.

4. Cut a piece of backing fabric the same size as the cushion front. Machine stitch the pieced front to the backing fabric, using a 1cm (⅜in) seam allowance.

5. For an envelope back, cut two pieces of fabric to the same height and two thirds of the width of the cushion front. Press under a double 1.5cm (⅝in) hem down one long side of each; machine stitch in place.

6. Pin the backs to the cushion front with right sides facing overlapping the hemmed edges to fit. Machine stitch all the way around with a 1.5cm (⅝in) seam allowance. Trim corners and turn through.

LAVENDER HEART
by Mary Fogg

You Will Need:

Fabric design roll
Kathy Davis Journeys

◆

White sewing thread
Gutermann colour 800

◆

Pink ribbon

◆

Dried lavender and toy filling

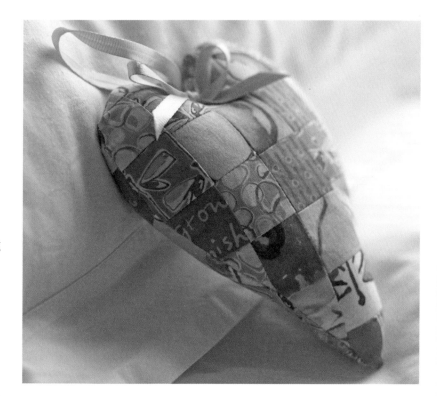

1. Make yourself a card template measuring 3.5cm (1⅜in) square, and use to cut out 70 squares in various patterns. Press the fabric squares. Lay out the squares in your preferred order to form a large rectangle of 10 rows, with seven squares top to bottom.

2. Take the first two squares in row 1 and with right sides facing stitch along the top edge. Add the third square, stitching along the bottom edge this time. Continue until you have finished your first row of seven squares. It may be helpful to number each strip 1–10 as you go.

3. Once all strips are sewn, press, then, with right sides facing, sew the first two strips together. Repeat until you have joined all 10 strips to form a piece of patchwork; gently press.

4. You now have a rectangle of patchwork from which to cut your heart shape. With right sides facing, fold the fabric in half, short sides together and pin. Place the heart template on the patchwork piece and draw around it with a pencil. This is your stitching line.

5. Starting half way along one side, machine stitch around the marked pencil line, taking great care with the curves, and leaving a 5cm (2in) gap for turning.

6. Cut out the heart shape 6mm (¼in) from the stitched line. Snip into the curves and down into the V to get the best possible shape, and turn right side out. Gently press into shape, stuff and add in some dried lavender. Sew the gap closed using slip stitch. Stitch a ribbon loop at the top of heart to hang.

PATCHWORK AND QUILTING

JUGGLING BALLS

by Upinder Birdi

You Will Need:

Fat quarter fabric pack
Kaffe Fassett

◆

Burgundy sewing thread
Gutermann colour 108

◆

100g (4oz) dried pulses for stuffing

1. The fabric you use for making the juggling balls must be a tight cotton weave and a fat quarter pack is perfect as it gives you a great selection of co-ordinating fabrics in complementary colourways. Choose four different colours and press flat.

2. Use the juggling ball template to cut four panels from each of your chosen fabrics; you will require four panels for each ball, but do not choose more than one of the same panel for any one ball.

3. Now start to piece the panel pieces for each ball together. Lay two panels on top of each other, right sides facing, and pin together. Taking a 1.3cm (½in) seam allowance, stitch along one edge following the shape of the curve; double stitch for extra security.

4. Repeat for the two remaining panels. Then pin the two joined panels together, right sides facing. Stitch around the edges so that the four panels are stitched together, leaving a gap for turning and stuffing of about 3cm (1⅛in). You now have an inside out flat ball.

5. Turn the ball the right way and poke out the edges with a pencil. Using a funnel, stuff the ball tightly with dried pulses.

6. Fold the edges of the turning gap neatly in and stitch closed using an invisible ladder stitch.

7. Repeat steps 3–6 to make two more balls.

QUILTED OVEN GLOVE
by Sarah Callard

You Will Need:

Fabric for glove and lining
Tanya Whelan Delilah Lulu
Rose Blue and Dots Red

◆

White sewing thread
Gutermann colour 800

◆

Insulating wadding (batting)

◆

Ribbon

1. Draw loosely around the shape of your hand adding an extra 5cm (2in) all around and making sure it comes as far down your wrist as you'd like. Cut this out to make your oven glove template.

2. Fold the fabric in half; place the template on the folded fabric and draw around it to give you a front and a back glove. Cut out. Also use the template to cut out front and back piece from the wadding and a front and back from the lining fabric.

3. Tack (baste) the matching top and lining fabric pieces together with the wadding sandwiched in the middle. Quilt – crisscross lines are simple and effective.

4. With right sides facing, pin the quilted front and back pieces together, adding a loop of ribbon between the layers, making sure that the looped ends are facing inwards. Machine stitch together taking extra care where the thumb meets the rest of the glove.

5. Snip into the seams around the thumb and turn the glove right way out.

6. Cut a 10cm (3⅞in) wide strip of the lining fabric to bind the raw edge of the glove. Fold the fabric strip in half and press. Open up the strip and place one raw edge to the raw edge of the glove and stitch about 1.3cm (½in) from the edge. Fold the strip back over to the inside of the glove, turn under and machine or hem stitch in place.

PATCHWORK AND QUILTING

FLICKERING STAR PILLOW

by Tacha Bruecher

You Will Need:

Fabric for cushion front:
One piece 39cm x 58cm
(15⅝in x 23¼in) (solid white)
One piece 14cm x 14cm
(5⅝in x 5⅝in) (A)
One piece 43cm x 15cm
(17¼in x 6in) (B)
One piece 53cm x 17cm
(21¼in x 6⅞in) (C)
One piece 53cm x 17cm
(21¼in x 6⅞in) (D)
One piece 15cm x 30cm
(6in x 12in) (E)

Tilda Cotton White, Dena Fishbein
Kumari Garden Chandra Blue, Kamal
Moss, Kamal Stone, Tanaya Blue and
Tarika Moss

Fabric for cushion lining:
One piece 60cm x 60cm
(24in x 24in)

Tilda Cotton White

◆

White sewing thread
Gutermann colour 800

◆

Wadding (batting)

1. Cut your fabrics as follows:

From solid white fabric:
Two squares 15cm (6in)
Four squares 9cm (3½in)
Eight squares 7.5cm (3in)
Eight rectangles 7.5cm x
14cm (3in x 5½in)

From fabric A:
One square 14cm (5½in)

From fabric B:
Two squares 15cm (6in)

From fabric C:
Four squares 7.5cm (3in)
Four rectangles 7.5cm x
14cm (3in x 5½in)

From fabric D:
Four squares 9cm (3½in)
Eight squares 7.5cm (3in)

From fabric E:
Eight squares 7.5cm (3in)

2. Make four flying geese units using eight fabric E 7.5cm (3in) squares and four of the white 7.5cm x 14cm (3in x 5½in) rectangles. Trim to 7.5cm x 14cm (3in x 5½in). Sew two units to the top and bottom of the fabric A 14cm (5½in) square. Sew a fabric C 7.5cm (3in) square to opposite sides of the remaining fabric E flying geese. Sew to the sides of the fabric A square.

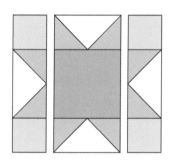

3. Make four flying geese units using eight fabric D 7.5cm (3in) squares and four of the white 7.5cm x 14cm (3in x 5½in) rectangles. Trim to 7.5cm x 14cm (3in x 5½in). Sew a white 7.5cm (3in) square to opposite side of each of the flying geese.

4. Make eight HSTs (half square triangles) using four fabric D 9cm (3½in) squares and four white 9cm (3½in) squares. Trim to 7.5cm (3in) square. Sew to opposite sides of the fabric C 7.5cm x 14cm (3in x 5½in) rectangles. Sew each of these units to the bottom of each of the fabric D flying geese units.

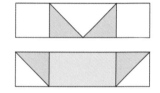

5. Sew two of the fabric D/C units to the top and bottom of the fabric A square.

6. Make four HSTs using two fabric B 15cm (6in) squares and two white 15cm (6in) squares. Trim to 14cm (5½in) square. Sew to opposite sides of two of the fabric D/C units. Sew to the sides of the fabric A square.

7. Layer the pillow top, wadding and lining fabric and tack (baste). Quilt as desired.

8. Finish the pillow using a backing of your choice. Bind the edges for a neat finish.

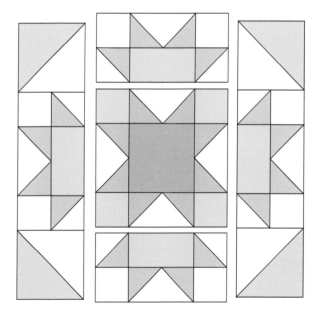

PATCHWORK AND QUILTING

PATCHWORK TABLE MAT

by Linda Clements

You Will Need:

Patterned fabric for mat top:
Ten pieces 7cm x 7cm
(2¾in x 2¾in)
Dena Fishbein Kumari Garden Jeevan
Blue, Lalit Blue, Marala Blue, Teja
Blue and Tara Stone

White fabric for mat top:
Two pieces 7cm x 29.8cm
(2¾in x 11¾in)

Fabric for mat centre and
backing:
One piece 16.5cm x 29.8cm
(8½in x 11¾in)
One piece 30.5cm x 45.7cm
(12in x 18in)
Dena Fishbein Kumari
Garden and Kamal Stone

◆

Wadding (batting):
One piece 30.5cm x 45.7cm
(12in x 18in)

◆

White sewing thread
Gutermann colour 800

◆

Blue, red-orange and green
stranded cotton (floss)
DMC colours 322, 350 and 320

1. To create the patchwork, take five of the 7cm (2¾in) print squares and using 6mm (¼in) seams, sew the squares together. Press seams in one direction. Do the same with the other five squares, changing the order if desired. Take the two strips of white fabric and sew one to the right side of one set of print squares and the other to the left side of the other set of print squares. Press the seams. Now take the pale print fabric piece, sew it to the white strips and press seams.

2. To hand quilt the mat, use the template provided. Copy the template and tape it to a bright window. Tape the patchwork on top, right side up, so the pattern shows through one of the white fabric strips. Use a pencil to lightly trace the pattern onto the fabric. Now copy the pattern onto the other white strip. Place the piece of wadding on the back of the patchwork and safety pin in place. Quilt through both layers using three strands of stranded cotton. Quilt the flower outlines in blue, the inner circle in red-orange and the linking curves in green. Stitch the central cross as long stitches in green.

3. To machine quilt the mat, press it first and then using thread to match the fabrics, quilt by machine down the long seams, 'in the ditch'. Press the work.

4. To finish the mat, place the patchwork right side up. Place the backing fabric right side down on top and pin together. Trim the wadding and backing to the same size as the patchwork. Sew the pieces together all the way around the edge leaving a gap of about 12.7cm (5in) in the bottom. Trim the points off the corners a little, turn through to the right side and press the seam.

5. Turn the edges of the gap inwards neatly and hand sew together with little stitches and matching thread. Finish by using your sewing machine to sew all around the edge of the mat about 3mm (1/8in) from the edge all round. This is called topstitching and creates a neat, firm edge.

PATCHWORK AND QUILTING

STRIPED TOTE BAG
by Mary Fogg

You Will Need:

Fat quarter fabric pack
Dena Fishbein Kumari Garden

◆

Fabric for bag lining:
Two pieces 30cm x 35cm
(11⅞in x 13⅞in)
Dena Fishbein Kumari
Garden Marala Pink

◆

White sewing thread
Gutermann colour 800

◆

Pink ribbon

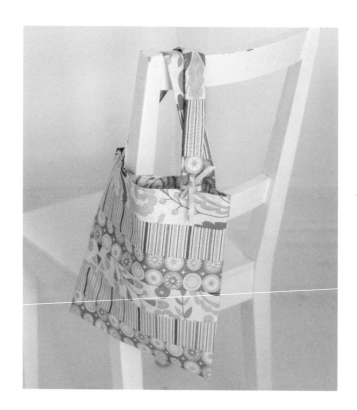

1. Choose three different fabrics and from each fabric piece, cut out four strips each measuring 30cm x 8cm (11⅞in x 3½in). You should end up with 12 strips in total, six for the front and six for the back of the bag. Decide on your preferred layout of the strips.

2. Allowing for a 6mm (¼in) seam allowance, pin the first two strips together, right sides facing. Machine stitch along the edge and continue in the same way adding each strip as you go, until the first six strips have been sewn to form the front of your bag. Press seams open on the reverse, then press the front. Repeat for the bag back.

3. Put the patchwork back and front together with right sides facing. Pin around the three sides making sure all seams match up, and leaving the top open. Machine stitch with a 6mm (¼in) seam allowance. Turn inside out and press in a 1.3cm (½in) hem at the top (wrong sides facing).

4. Place the lining pieces together with right sides facing. Pin then machine stitch together just as you did for the main bag following step 3.

5. Put the lining in the main bag; align pressed hems at the top; pin.

6. To make the handles cut 12 9cm x 9cm (3½in x 3½in) pieces (six per handle) and make a patchwork strip (see step 2). Press in half, long sides together and open. Press a 1cm (⅜in) hem along each long side and fold strip over so hems meet; pin, then sew. Place the straps in between the lining and main bag so they are the same distance from the sides; pin. Topstitch all the way around the top edge of the bag.

HEARTS CUSHION
by Jenny Arnott

You Will Need:

Fabrics for cushion front:
Tilda Christmas House Big Spot Red,
Flower Ornament Red on White,
Little Flower Burgundy, Rose White,
Dots Red, Red Stripe and Betsy Pink

Fabric for cushion back:
One piece 25cm x 39cm
(9⅞in x 15⅜in)
One piece 28cm x 39cm
(11in x 15⅜in)
Tilda Gingham Pink

◆

Red and pink sewing thread
Gutermann colours 909 and 660

◆

1m (1¼yd) lightweight
interlining

1. Make a square template from card measuring 8.5cm x 8.5cm (3⅜in x 3⅜in). Iron interlining onto the back of your patterned Tilda fabrics, then use the template to cut out 25 squares. Arrange the squares in a 5 x 5 grid.

2. Using the template, cut a heart from card and use to cut out 13 hearts from your fabrics.

3. Place the hearts on alternate squares; stitch using red thread.

4. Place two squares together with right sides facing. Machine stitch down one vertical edge with a 6mm (¼in) seam allowance. Press the seam open. Work along the row until all five squares are joined in a line. Repeat for the next four rows, then stitch all five rows together in the same way to form a square. Press the seams open.

5. To make the envelope back, first fold over and stitch a narrow double hem down one long edge of each cushion back piece.

6. With right sides facing, pin the hemmed rectangles to the cushion front with the hemmed edges overlapping. Machine stitch together around the sides with a 6mm (¼in) seam allowance, using light pink thread. Remove the pins, then trim the corners to reduce bulk. Turn your finished cushion cover the right way out through the envelope back. Press and insert a 38cm (15in) cushion pad.

SEWING

BOW MAKE-UP PURSE
by Marion Elliot

You Will Need:

Fabric for bag, lining
and bow:
One piece 35cm x 35cm
(13⅞in x 13⅞in)
One piece 35cm x 35cm
(13⅞in x 13⅞in)
Two pieces 11cm x 40cm
(4⅜in x 15½in)
Amy Butler Soul Blossoms Laurel
Dots Periwinkle, Laurel Dots
Cherry and Laurel Dots Cilantro

◆

Blue sewing thread
Gutermann colour 825

◆

Medium fusible interlining

1. Using the pattern, cut a purse front and back from periwinkle fabric and two linings from cherry fabric. Iron the interlining to the reverse of the front and back.

2. Take the cilantro fabric strips, and press under and machine hem the long sides. Machine one end of each tie to the sides of the purse front. Hem the free ends. Stitch along the middle of each tie for 11cm (4⅜in) from the side of the purse front. Tie the ends in a bow.

3. Pin the top of the purse front, face down, to the upper edge of the zip, lining up the raw edge with the top of the zip. Tack (baste) in place. Pin the top of the purse back to the lower edge of the zip as before and tack (baste).

4. Machine stitch the zip in place; remove the tacking (basting). Place the purse right side up. Attach the zipper foot. Open the zip halfway, then stitch along both sides of the zip, close to the turned edge.

5. Pin the purse front and back together, with right sides facing, pinning a ribbon loop between the side seams, pointing in. Machine stitch leaving the top edge open. Press open seams.

6. Press corners flat, aligning base and side seams. Measure in 2cm (¾in) at either side and stitch vertically across the corners; trim. Turn through. Repeat to make lining. Insert lining into the purse and slip stitch in place just below zip.

FUN APRON

by Hannah Kelly

You Will Need:

Fabric for apron:
One piece 100cm x 60cm
(40in x 24in)
LoulouThi Laminated
Summer Totem Tart

Fabric for pocket and ties:
One piece 20cm x 20cm
(7⅞in x 7⅞in)
Three pieces 50cm x 4cm
(20in x 1½in)
LoulouThi Laminated Stockings Twist

◆

Black sewing thread
Gutermann colour 190

1. Cut the arm shapes from the floral fabric leaving a 20cm (7⅞in) width across the top of the fabric and 25cm (9⅞in) in length from the top. Machine stitch with an overlock stitch all around the edge of the apron.

2. Take the fabric strips and fold each in half with right sides facing; sew along one end and the long edge to leave one end open. Turn right side out. Fold in the edges of the open ends and hand stitch closed.

3. Sew the two waist ties and the necktie in place at the edges of the apron. Adjust the length of the necktie for personal preference.

4. Fold the edges of the pocket in by 1cm (⅜in). Sew along the top edge of the pocket, and then sew the prepared pocket onto the apron in your preferred position.

5. Make sure you leave the pocket top open and be sure to catch the folded edges of the pocket with your stitches.

SEWING

COFFEE POT COSY
by Charlotte Addison

You Will Need:

Fabric for cosy:
One piece 114cm x 50cm
(45½in x 20in)
Free Spirit Designer Solids Red

Fabric for lining and appliqué
One piece 114cm x 50cm
(45½in x 20in)
Tanya Whelan Delilah Dots Blue

◆

Red ribbon

◆

Medium sew-in interlinining

◆

Fusible webbing

◆

White sewing thread
Gutermann colour 800

1. Enlarge the coffee pot cosy template and cut out two of each (a front and a back) from the cosy fabric, the lining fabric and the interlining. Trace the heart template four times onto fusible webbing and roughly cut out the heart shapes. Iron onto the appliqué fabric and cut out neatly. Remove the backing paper from the motifs and position them, glue side down, onto the cosy front and back, placing one above the other centrally.

2. Place the cosy front and back together with right sides facing and pin. Take 5cm (2in) of ribbon, fold in half and place in between fabric at the centre top, loop facing inwards. Re-pin. Machine stitch with a 6mm (¼in) seam allowance. Turn right side out and press.

3. Place two lining pieces together, right sides facing, and place between the two interlinings.

4. Sew around the edge leaving the bottom open. Put the cosy inside the lining, right sides facing, and align raw edges. Pin, then stitch around the bottom edge leaving a 7.5cm (3in gap). Turn right side out and press.

5. Fold in the edges of the turning gap and pin. Topstitch around the bottom of the cosy about 1.3cm (½in) from the edge. Press.

SEWING

FABRIC BOOKMARK
by Hannah Kelly

You Will Need:

Fabric for bookmark:
One piece 20cm x 10cm
(7⅞in x 3⅞in)
Amy Butler Love Memeno Burgundy

◆

Black sewing thread
Gutermann colour 190

◆

Thick white card

1. Cut out a rectangular piece of thick white card to measure 16cm x 4cm (6⅜in x 1½in).

2. With the fabric laid out right side up on your work surface, place the cardboard on top of the left edge of the fabric leaving a 1cm (⅜in) edge. Fold the rest of the fabric over the card, pulling it tight. (The pattern on the fabric should be on the inside now.)

3. Sew along the outer edges of the fabric, as close to the card edge as possible, ensuring the material is pulled tight along the folded side. Leave one end open at the top. Cut off any excess material along the edges.

4. Remove the piece of card and turn the fabric inside out so that the pattern is now right side out. Push the card back inside.

5. Fold the open edges neatly and hand sew the final edge. Using a zigzag stitch, machine stitch about 6mm (¼in) from the edge of the bookmark all the way around.

SEWING

ROLLED FELT ROSE CORSAGE
by Jane Millard

You Will Need:

Pink and green felt

◆

Light green sewing thread
Gutermann colour 153

◆

Brooch back

1. Cut a 15cm (6in) diameter pink felt circle and cut into a spiral.

2. Roll up the spiral from the outside edge to form the flower; keep the centre tight and loosen near the end to create a rose. Stitch the end to secure beneath the flower.

3. Cut two leaves and backstitch around the edges and through the centre with light green sewing thread for the veins.

4. Secure the leaves under the flower with a few neat stitches.

5. Cut a small circle of pink felt to cover the raw edges at the back of the flower and stitch in place. Stitch the finished rose onto the brooch back.

SEWING

ELEPHANT TOY
by Denise Mutton

You Will Need:

Fabric for elephant
body and ears/tail
Tanya Whelan Delilah Amelie Pink
and Tanya Whelan Delilah Dots Red

◆

Toy filling

◆

Medium iron-on interlining

◆

Two small buttons

1. Trace off the patterns and use to cut out 2 x A (body), 2 x B (head and trunk), 2 x C (legs) from one fabric, and 4 x D (ear) and 1 x E (tail) from a contrasting fabric. Fold your fabrics in half before pinning patterns in place and cutting out (to ensure pattern pieces are reversed as necessary).

2. When sewing your fabric pieces together, always have the right sides of the fabric facing. Before turning sewn fabric pieces through to the right side, snip curved seams close to the stitching line taking care not to cut through the sewn stitches.

3. Turn a narrow hem on the long ends of the tail, fold wrong sides facing to bring the hemmed edges together and sew. Knot one end.

4. Using D, cut two ears from interlining. Place two patterned fabric ear pieces together, right sides facing and sandwich an interlining in between. Sew around the curved edges only; turn through and press. Pin an ear to each body piece, aligning raw edges and sew in place.

5. Tack (baste) the legs to the body and sew. Now sew the leg sections together along the straight edge.

6. Sew the head/trunk sections to the body, taking care to keep the legs out of the way. Pin the tail in place facing inwards, and sew the sides together stitching only up to where the legs are sewn – leave a gap for stuffing. Turn right side out, firmly stuff and ladder stitch to close gap. Sew on button eyes.

SEWING

CHILDREN'S LAUNDRY BAG
by Lisa Fordham

You Will Need:

Fabric for bag:
One piece 60cm x 45cm
(24in x 18in)
Tanya Whelan Delilah Paisley Blue

◆

Mother-of-pearl buttons

◆

1.5m (1¾yd) cord

◆

Pink felt

◆

Stranded cotton (floss)
or yarn

1. Fold the fabric in half widthways, right sides facing; pin. Sew the sides together.

2. Make a channel at the top of the bag for the drawstring. Fold over the edge by 1cm (⅜in), press, then fold over again by 4cm (1½in). Pin, tack (baste), press. Stitch along the bottom edge of the folded fabric only, ensuring the channel is large enough to thread your cord through and leaving a 2cm (¾in) gap.

3. Turn the laundry bag right side out and thread the cord through the gap in the stitched channel.

4. Cut a simple shaped name label out of pink felt (approximately 15cm/6in or longer if necessary). Use tailor's chalk to sketch out the child's name then hand embroider over your outline using a decorative stitch of your choice (chain stitch for example) in stranded cotton or yarn as you prefer.

5. Pin the name label to the bag front and sew in place using a simple running stitch. Cut a wiggly line from the felt long enough to reach from the name label to the top of the bag. Pin and stitch through the centre of the shape. Add buttons to the name label for decoration.

CUTE FABRIC CUPCAKES
by Debbie Pyne

You Will Need:

Scraps of fabric for cupcakes
Dena Fishbein Kumari Garden Sashi
Pink, Jeevan Blue and Chandra Red

◆

Two sheets of white felt

◆

Pink sewing thread
Gutermann colour 321

◆

Pastel seed beads

◆

Coloured buttons
Zippity Do-Dah

◆

Silk ribbons

◆

Wadding (batting)

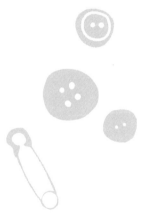

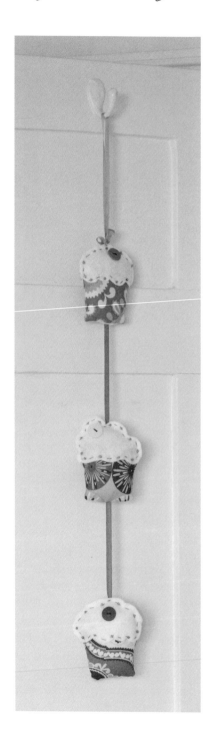

1. Using the templates cut out six cupcake cases from patterned fabric and six icing pieces from white felt. Stitch a button onto the right side of each piece of felt icing.

2. Using running stitch and pink sewing thread, hand stitch a felt icing piece onto each cupcake case, stitching along the bottom edge of the icing only and threading a seed bead onto the thread on every other stitch.

3. Place the cupcake cases together with right sides facing. To join the cupcakes into a string for hanging, place a length of silk ribbon at the middle of the bottom edge. Machine stitch together with a narrow seam allowance, from just beneath the icing piece around the sides and bottom edge, stopping when you meet the icing again at the other side. Turn right sides out.

4. Continue to hand stitch the icing together as in step 2, remembering to sew in a ribbon piece at the top for connecting to the next cupcake in the string, and stuffing with a little wadding before completely sewing up the icing.

SEWING

SUFFOLK PUFF NECKLACE
by Dorothy Wood

You Will Need:

Fat quarter fabric pack
Dena Designs Kumari Garden

◆

Pink and baby blue felt

◆

50cm (20in) silver chain

◆

Silver jump rings

◆

Silver clasp

◆

Mother-of-pearl buttons

1. Draw three circles onto the reverse side of the fabric twice the size you need for each puff – 8cm (3½in) diameter is a good size. Cut out along the lines.

2. Tie a knot on the end of a length of sewing thread. Stitch around the edge of a fabric circle using a small running stitch. Pull the thread to gather the fabric to create a puff and sew in the ends to secure.

3. Draw a 2cm (¾in) diameter circle onto the pink and blue felt.

4. Cut just inside the line using ordinary scissors for one circle; cut the other circle out just outside the line with pinking shears.

5. Layer the felt onto the gathered side of the puff and sew a small button in place. Repeat to make two more embellished puffs.

6. Stitch the puffs onto a 50cm (20in) length of chain. Stitch with the chain going across above the middle so that the puffs hang flat and don't fall forward. Use a jump ring to attach the fastening to one end of the chain and add a jump ring at the other end to finish.

SEWING

CAT PINCUSHION BRACELET
by Zoe Larkins

You Will Need:

Scraps of fabric
for pincushion
Tanya Whelan Delilah Paisley Blue

◆

Pink, sandstone
and white felt

◆

Two large mother-
of-pearl buttons

◆

White and black
sewing thread

◆

Thick elastic cord

◆

Beads

◆

Toy filling

1. Using the template, cut out two cat head shapes from the patterned fabric. Use the felt to make a face on one of the head shapes: cut two circles of white felt for the cheeks, a little pink heart for the nose, and a sandstone triangle for the forehead/bridge of the nose.

2. Use white thread and slip stitch to sew on the felt face.

3. Sew on the two large mother-of-pearl buttons with black thread for the cat's eyes.

4. Pin the two head shapes together, with right sides facing. Machine stitch all the way around the edge with a 6mm (¼in) seam allowance, leaving a small gap at the bottom for turning. Stuff the head and neatly stitch the gap closed.

5. Cut a piece of elastic to fit your wrist, and thread beads on to make a bracelet. Stitch the bracelet onto the back of the head. Wear your pincushion bracelet as you sew, sticking your pins into your cat's cheeks to look like whiskers!

SEWING

EGG COSIES
by Marion Elliot

You Will Need:

Small pieces of fabric
Tilda Christmas House Grandma
Rose Red, Christmas House Big
Spot Pink, Christmas House Big
Spot Red and Tammie Pink

◆

Fusible webbing

◆

Small pieces of
narrow ribbon

◆

White sewing thread
Gutermann colour 800

1. Trace and transfer the egg cosy template to your chosen fabrics and cut out to make front, back and linings. Cut a contrasting panel for the front. Machine stitch the contrasting panel and ribbon trim to the egg cosy front.

2. Place the front and back, right sides up, onto the glue side of the fusible webbing and cut out roughly. Place a clean cloth over and press to attach the webbing. Trim neatly.

3. Pin the cosy front and back together, right sides facing. Insert and pin a loop of ribbon between the top seams, facing inwards.

4. Machine stitch together, using a 1cm (⅜in) seam allowance. Trim the seams and turn through the cosy to the right side. Pin the lining front and back together and machine stitch around the sides using a 1cm (⅜in) seam allowance. Trim seams. Leave the lining inside out.

5. Pull the lining over the cosy, then pin the lower edges together, matching raw edges. Machine stitch around the lower edge, leaving an gap to turn the cosy through. Turn through, then slip stitch the opening closed, using small, neat stitches.

SEWING

RETRO PINNY

by Rowena Lane

You Will Need:

Fat quarter fabric pack
Amy Butler Soul Blossoms

◆

Blue sewing thread
Gutermann colour 827

1. Cut out a rectangle 51cm x 56cm (20⅜in x 22⅜in) from one of the fat quarters. Choosing a contrast fabric, cut out a 17cm (6⅝in) square for the pocket.

2. Hem the pocket piece on each side with a double hem: fold over by 1cm (⅜in), press, fold over by 1cm (⅜in) and press again. Topstitch the pocket onto the apron body 12cm (4¾in) from the top edge and 9cm (3½in) in from the side.

3. Hem the apron body on each side with a double hem, using a 1.5cm (⅝in) turnover this time. Make a row of running stitches to gather in 2cm (¾in) down from top edge. Draw up thread to gather waist to 36cm (14¼in).

4. Cut two contrast fabric ties 10cm (3⅞in) by the length of the longest edge of the fat quarter. Cut the waistband strip 10cm x 37cm (3⅞in x 14⅝in). Join the strips, with the waist strip in the centre. Press seams open. Turn over a 1.5cm (⅝in) hem all round and press.

5. To attach the waistband unfold the top fold line and place right side down on the right side of the top edge of the apron body; pin.

6. Sew along the gathering line. Fold the strip back over. Turn in the ends of each tie and topstitch the folded fabric on the open edges of both ties. Slip stitch the waistband section to the wrong side of the apron.

7. Turn up the hem at the bottom edge of the apron as required and hem stitch in place.

TABLE RUNNER
by Lisa Fordham

You Will Need:

Fabric for runner
back, front and ends:
One piece 38cm x 95cm
(15in x 37¼in)
Two pieces 10cm x 95cm
(3⅞in x 37¼in)
Two pieces 25cm x 85cm
(9⅞in x 33⅜in)
Tanya Whelan Delilah Dots Blue

Fabric for runner
front panel:
One piece 18cm x 95cm
(15in x 37¼in)
Tanya Whelan Delilah Dots Blue

◆

Purple cotton lace and
narrow satin ribbon

◆

Four large white buttons

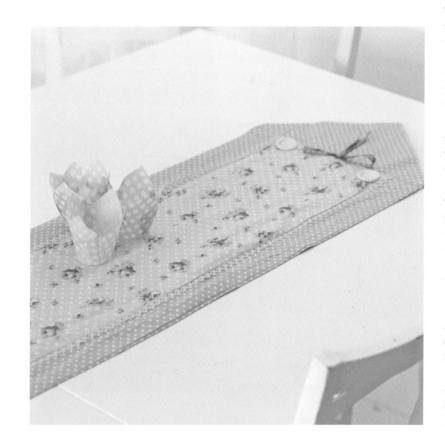

1. To make the front, lay the blue buds strip between the 10cm (3⅞in) wide strips of blue dots; pin and tack (baste) . Lay the lace over the top where the strips join and machine stitch together on both sides.

2. Fold over the long edges of the pieced front and the 38cm (15in) wide blue dots back piece. Place the front and back together with wrong sides facing; pin, tack (baste) and machine stitch.

3. To make the pointed ends, take the remaining two pieces of blue dot fabric and fold widthways to the width of your runner. Fold in the edges on both sides and press. Fold over the bottom edge and press.

4. Fold the corners over to the centre back, press again and machine stitch to the runner at either end folding in untidy edges as you go. Hand stitch the corner points in position on the reverse.

5. Cut two lengths of ribbon approximately 80cm (31⅜in) long and tie into large bows. Pin and hand sew to each end of runner. Add the buttons to corners of the blue buds panel to finish.

SEWING

MINI COCKTAIL-PARTY HAT
by Jennifer Grace

You Will Need:

Fabric for hat
Tanya Whelan Delilah Bijou
Pink and Dots Pink

◆

Toy filling

◆

Firm iron-on interlining

◆

Light pink sewing thread
Gutermann colour 320

◆

Checked pink satin ribbon

1. From floral fabric cut an 18cm x 12cm (7in x 4¾in) rectangle, and a 7cm (2¾in) circle. Fold the rectangle in half, right sides facing, so the short edges meet and sew together with a 1cm (⅜in) seam. Press seam flat. This forms the main upright section of the hat.

2. Draw a 5cm (2in) circle in the centre of the larger circle; snip notches towards the inner circle. With right sides facing, sew to the top of the upright section along the drawn circle, keeping the ease even.

3. Put a 4.5cm (1⅝in) diameter circle of white card into the top, turn piece right sides out and fill with toy filling.

4. Cut two 11cm (4⅜in) diameter circles from polka dot fabric. Cut two 9cm (3½in) diameter circles of interlining and iron to the centre of wrong side of each polka dot circle. Cut notches approximately 6mm (¼in) apart from the raw edges of the circles towards the interlining. Fold the notched edges into the middle and press.

5. Make small snips around the base of the upright hat section; fold inwards. Sew the upright section to the centre right side of a polka dot circle. Cut a 115cm (45in) length of ribbon and sew it at its middle to the centre of the right side of the other polka dot circle, stopping 1.5cm (⅝in) from the brim either side.

6. Sew together the two polka dot circles wrong sides facing and snipped edges folded in, stitching close to the edge. To finish tie ribbon in a bow around the brim.

SEWING

FELT PARTY BAGS
by Katy Denny

You Will Need:

Green and purple felt
30cm x 22cm
(11⅞in x 8⅝in)

◆

Green and purple
sewing thread
Gutermann colours 585 and 463

◆

Flower sequins

◆

Assorted bright ribbons

◆

Silicone glue

1. To give you two rectangles 15cm x 22cm (6in x 8⅝in), cut a felt rectangle in half across its length.

2. Choose a ribbon that co-ordinates with your felt and cut it so that it is approximately 30cm (11⅞in) long.

3. Fold your felt rectangle in half Pin the sides together and hand-or machine-stitch the side seams.

4. Take your ribbon and sew one end to the top left of the bag, taking care to only sew through one layer of felt. Turn the bag over and sew the other end of the ribbon to the top left of that side.

5. Turn your bag the right way out and push out the bottom corners with a pencil. Use a dab of silicone glue to stick the flower sequins randomly across the front and the back of the bag.

SEWING

FANCY FABRIC CORSAGE
by Kirsty Neale

You Will Need:

Fabric for corsage
Four pieces approximately
20cm x 20cm (8in x 8in)
Tilda Christmas House Big Spot
Pink, Tilda Christmas House
Grandma Rose Red, Tilda Berrie
Pink and Amy Butler Lotus
Full Moon Polka Dot Lime

◆

Decorative brad
Tilda Fruit Garden

◆

Brown felt

◆

Brooch back

1. Using the petal template, draw around it onto the reverse of your chosen fabrics. You will need 8–10 petal pieces for your fancy fabric corsage. Cut out.

2. Scrunch each petal piece between your hands to roughen and deliberately fray the edges. Layer the pieces one on top of the other, staggering the petals as you go.

3. To fix them together, draw a small circle onto the back of the petal stack. Sew a line of simple running stitches around the circle. Pull the thread ends together, gathering up the fabric very slightly. Knot to secure.

4. Use your hands to 'fluff' the gently gathered petals and give your corsage shape.

5. Fix a decorative brad on top of the petals to make a flower centre.

6. To finish off, cut a circle of felt and stitch to the back of your corsage. Sew a brooch back onto the felt.

SEWING

SIMPLE SHOPPING BAG
by Marion Elliot

You Will Need:

Fabric for bag front, back and handles:
Two pieces 43cm x 38cm (16⅝in x 15in)
Two pieces 60cm x 12cm (23¾in x 4¾in)
Tilda Oval Rose Green

Fabric for bag lining:
Two pieces 43cm x 38cm (16⅝in x 15in)
Tilda Spot Pink

Fabric for purse front, back and lining:
Four pieces 12cm x 14cm (4¾in x 5½in)
Tilda Rosalie Red

◆

10cm (3⅞in) zip

1. Pin bag front and back with right sides facing. Pin a ribbon loop facing inwards between the side seams. Sew sides and base using a 1.5cm (⅝in) seam allowance; trim corners, turn through. Make the lining but do not turn through.

2. Press a 1cm (⅜in) hem along the handle length, press in half lengthwise, wrong sides facing. Oversew handles down both sides (1cm/⅜in seam allowance. Pin to the bag front and back, handles down, raw edges matching. Sew.

3. Insert the main bag inside the lining and pin the top edges together, matching the seams exactly and keeping the handles to the inside. Sew around the top of the bag (1.5cm/⅝in seam allowance), with a gap to turn the bag through. Turn the bag through, press and slip stitch the gap closed. Overstitch around top of bag. Attach a split ring to the loop.

4. Pin and tack (baste) the top of the purse front, face down, to the top of the zip, lining up the raw edges.

5. Pin and tack (baste) the top of the purse back to the lower edge of the zip. Sew both sides of the zip in place, then remove tacking. Place the purse right side up and stitch along both sides of zip (zipper foot).

6. Pin ribbon loop between the side seams of the purse. Sew sides and base together, right sides facing. Trim corners, turn through. Make a lining, turn through. Press under raw edges. Place lining inside purse and slip stitch in place just below zip. Attach a D ring to the loop.

TECHNIQUES

CROCHET

Crochet abbreviations

Be aware that crochet terms in the US are different from those in the UK. This can be confusing as the same terms are used to refer to different stitches under each system. All crochet patterns in this book use UK terminology. The list here gives abbreviations and a translation of UK terms to US terms:

UK term	US term
chain (ch)	chain
double crochet (dc)	single crochet
half treble (htr)	half double crochet
treble (tr)	double crochet
double treble (dtr)	treble crochet
slip stitch (sl st)	slip stitch

slip knot

double crochet

treble

Granny squares

To make a granny square, follow the basic pattern below:

Foundation round: Make 4 ch and join with a sl st to form a ring.

Rnd 1: (RS) 3ch (counts as first tr), 2tr into ring, (2ch, 3tr into ring) 3 times, 1htr into top of 3ch at beg of round.

Rnd 2: 3ch (counts as first tr), (2tr, 2ch and 3tr) into first ch sp, *2ch, miss 3tr, (3tr, 2ch and 3tr) into next ch sp, rep from * twice more, miss 3tr, 1htr into top of 3ch at beg of round.

Rnd 3: 3ch (counts as first tr), 2tr into first ch sp, *2ch, miss 3tr, (3tr, 2ch and 3tr) into next ch sp**, 2ch, miss 3tr, 3tr into next ch sp, rep from * to end, ending last rep at **, miss 3tr, 1htr into top of 3ch at beg of round.

Rnd 4: 3ch (counts as first tr), 2tr into first ch sp, 2ch, miss 3tr, 3tr into next ch sp, *2ch, miss 3tr, (3tr, 2ch and 3tr) into next ch sp**, (2ch, miss 3tr, 3tr into next ch sp) twice, rep from * to end, ending last rep at **, miss 3tr, 1htr into top of 3ch at beg of round. Continue in this way until your granny square is the desired size.
Fasten off.

slip stitch

chain

half treble

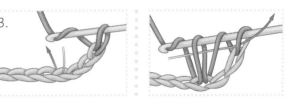

KNITTING

Knitting abbreviations

Abbreviations are used in knitting patterns to shorten commonly used terms so that the instructions are easier to read and a manageable length. The following is a list of the abbreviations you need to make the projects in this book. All knitting patterns in this book use UK terminology. The tinted panel below lists the most common differences between US and UK knitting terms.

beg.................. beginning
BL .... backward loop
C .... contrasting colour
cm.................. centimetre(s)
cont .... continue
dec(s) .... decrease/decreasing
DK .... double knitting
dpn.................. double-pointed needles
g .... gram(s)
inc.................. increase(s)/increasing
in(s) .... inch(es)
k.................... knit
k2tog............. knit 2 stitches together (1 stitch decreased)
k3tog............. knit 3 stitches together (2 stitches decreased)
k2tog tbl .... knit 2 stitches together through back of loops (1 stitch decreased)
kf&b............... knit into front and back of stitch (1 stitch increased)
LH .... left hand
m.................... metre(s)
MC .... main colour
mm.................. millimetres
oz .... ounces
p.................... purl
patt(s) .... pattern(s)
pfb .... purl into front and back of stitch (to increase by 1 stitch)
prev................ previous
psso............... pass slipped stitches over
p2tog .... purl 2 stitches together (1 stitch decreased)
rem .... remain/remaining
rep(s) .... repeat(s)

RH.................. right hand
rnd .... round
RS .... right side
sl.................... slip
sl st .... slip stitch
sp(s) .... space(s)
st st .... stockinette (stocking) stitch (1 row k, 1 row p)
st(s) .... stitch(es)
tbl .... through back of loop
tog .... together
WS .... wrong side
yd(s)............... yards(s)
yfwd............... yarn forward
yo .... yarn over
* .... repeat directions following * as many times as indicated or to end of row
( ).................... repeat instructions in round brackets

knitting terms

UK term	US term
stocking stitch	stockinette stitch
reverse stocking stitch	reverse stockinette stitch
moss stitch	seed stitch
double moss stitch or seed stitch	moss stitch
cast off	bind off
tension	gauge

cast on

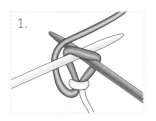   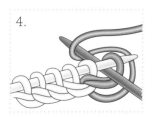

knit stitch

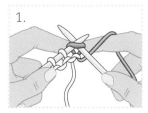   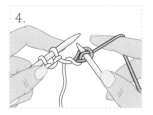

knit stitch (continental)

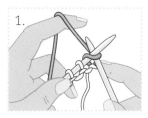 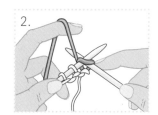  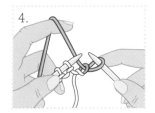

purl stitch

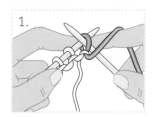 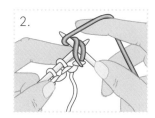 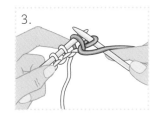 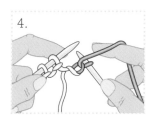

purl stitch (continental)

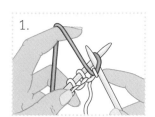 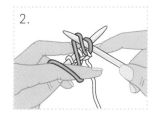 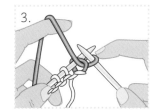 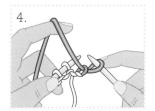

TECHNIQUES

Knitting in the round

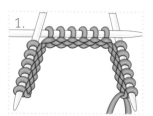

Grafting

Working from right to left, insert the tapestry needle from the back of the work through the first stitch on each edge and pull the yarn through. Continue in this way, forming a new row of stitches.

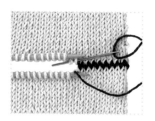

I-cord

1. Cast on a small number of stitches on a circular or double-pointed needle. Push the stitches to the other end of the needle and turn the needle, so the first stitch you'll knit is the first one you cast on.

2. Knit the stitches, making sure you pull the yarn tight for the first stitch. Move the stitches to the other end of the needle. Repeat this process until the i-cord is the desired length.

Changing yarn colour

Insert the tip of the right-hand needle into the next stitch, place the cut end of the new colour over the old colour and over the tip of the right-hand needle. Take the working end of the new colour and knit the next stitch, pulling the cut end off the needle over the working end as the stitch is formed so it is not knitted in. Hold the cut end down against the back of the work. Once you've joined in all the colours that you need across the row, on the return row twist the yarns to join the blocks of colour together. When you change colour, always pick up the new colour from under the old yarn.

k2tog	p2tog	kf&b	Swiss darning
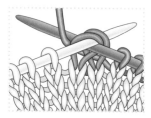			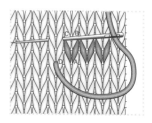

casting off

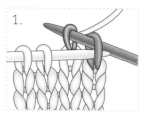

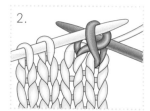

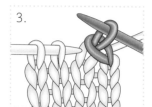

TECHNIQUES

SEWING

Basic stitches

When sewing by hand choose a needle that matches the thickness of the thread you are using, so the thread passes easily through the fabric. All stitches can be started with a knot on the back of the work and finished off neatly at the back, usually with backstitch.

backstitch

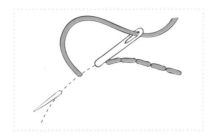

running stitch

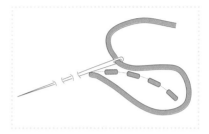

cross stitch

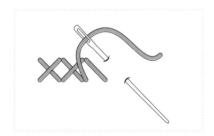

blanket stitch

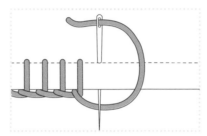

satin stitch

whip stitch

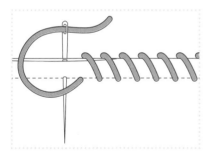

hem stitch

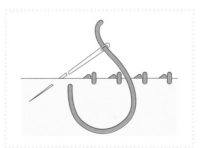

ladder stitch

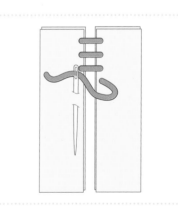

slip stitch

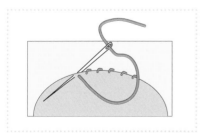

topstitch

TECHNIQUES

KNITTING CHARTS

Knitting charts are read from the bottom upwards. Each square represents a stitch. Read the odd rows (knit rows) from right to left and the even rows (purl rows) from left to right.

Busy Bee Cushion

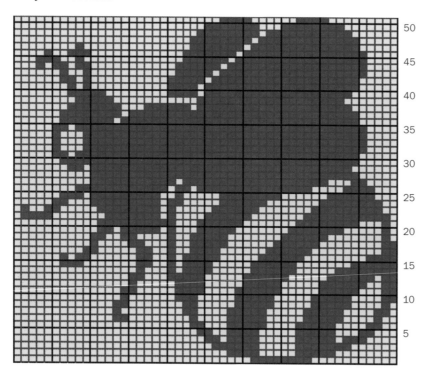

Kitten Mittens (Swiss darning chart)

Each square on the chart represents one knitted stitch 'v' shaped stitch, each line represents a straight stitch which runs diagonally across a stitch. And is worked after the squares have been darned in.

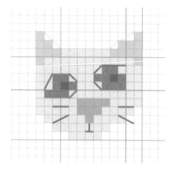

Camera Book Cover

Pretty Peg Bag

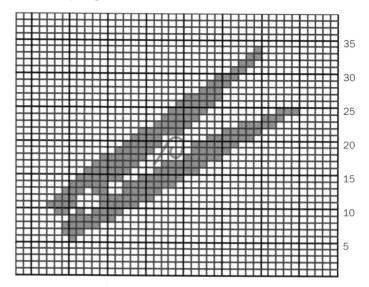

All other templates for the projects in this book can be found at:
www.stitchcraftcreate.com

SUPPLIERS

Materials to make the projects in this book can be found at:
www.rucraft.co.uk

ACKNOWLEDGMENTS

The publishers would like to thank all of the contributors
whose designs have been featured in this book:

Charlotte Addison	Mary Fogg	Jane Millard
Jenny Arnott	Lisa Fordham	Denise Mutton
Upinder Birdi	Jennifer Forster	Alison Myer
James Brooks	Claire Garland	Kirsty Neale
Tacha Bruecher	Jennifer Grace	Fiona-Grace Peppler
Ali Burdon	Verity Graves-Morris	Debbie Pyne
Louise Butt	Grace Harvey	Fiona Rinaldi
Sarah Callard	Jeni Hennah	Prudence Rogers
Ruth Clemens	Jo Irving	Jayne Schofield
Linda Clements	Hannah Kelly	Zoe Scott
Katy Denny	Ellen Kharade	Sue Trevor
Katherine Dyer	Rowena Lane	Lynda Wainwright
Marion Elliot	Nicola Langdon	Laura Whitcher
Sue Ellis	Zoe Larkins	Dorothy Wood

INDEX

LOVED THIS BOOK?

For more inspiration, ideas and free downloadable projects visit
www.stitchcraftcreate.com

TILDA'S SPRING IDEAS

Tone Finnanger

ISBN-13: 978-14463-0244-6

A gorgeous collection of fresh sewing projects using the latest Tilda fabrics and embellishments. Choose from a stunning variety of sewing and papercraft designs, including bags, soft toys, fabric boxes and unique decorations. The projects are accompanied by clear instructions, gorgeous photographs and colour illustrations.

HAPPY STITCH

Jodie Rackley

ISBN-13: 978-1-4403-1857-3

Charming felt and fabric projects that take minutes to make! With a few simple stitches and some basic materials, you'll be crafting in no time at all. From plush animals to electronics cozies and curtains to pillows, you'll love filling your home with bright and colorful crafty creations!

MAKE ME I'M YOURS... JUST FOR FUN

Various

ISBN-13: 978-1-4463-0069-5

Create 20 unique gifts and accessories, from jewellery and bags to socks and photo frames! Try your hand at a wide range of crafts, including sewing, knitting, crochet, papercraft, needle felting and soap making.

STITCH LONDON

Lauren O'Farrell

ISBN-13: 978-0-7153-3867-4

Whether you're just visiting or striving to survive as a city knitter, Stitch London is the place for you. And if you can't knit? Fear not! We'll even show you how to get clicking with your sticks and string.